ESCAPE TO
Morocco

Photography by Simon Russell
Text by Pamela Windo

Fodor's

FODOR'S TRAVEL PUBLICATIONS
NEW YORK • TORONTO • LONDON • SYDNEY • AUCKLAND • WWW.FODORS.COM

First Edition
ISBN 0-679-00515-3
ISSN 1528-3089

Special Sales
Fodor's Travel Publications are available at special discounts for bulk purchases for sales promotions or premiums. Special editions, including personalized covers, excerpts of existing guides, and corporate imprints, can be created in large quantities for special needs. For more information, contact your local bookseller or write to Special Markets, Fodor's Travel Publications, 201 E. 50th Street, New York, NY 10022. Inquiries from Canada should be directed to your local Canadian bookseller or sent to Random House of Canada, Ltd., Marketing Dept., 2775 Matheson Boulevard East, Mississauga, Ontario L4W 4P7. Inquiries from the United Kingdom should be sent to Fodor's Travel Publications, 20 Vauxhall Bridge Road, London, England SW1V 2SA.

PRINTED IN THE UNITED STATES OF AMERICA
10 9 8 7 6 5 4 3 2 1

Library of Congress Cataloging-in-Publication Data is available upon request.

Acknowledgments

The author and photographer warmly thank Mustapha Benkirane at Royal Air Maroc for magic carpet rides, Mohammed Marrakchi Ben Jaafar and Hind Amar at the Moroccan Tourist Office for their goodwill, David Rajwan and Josh Weiss at Spectra Photo Digital for processing a mountain of film, all the wonderful hotels cited within for hot meals and comfy beds, and Fabrizio La Rocca for his passionate vision.

Credits

Creative Director and Series Editor: Fabrizio La Rocca
Editorial Director: Karen Cure
Art Director: Tigist Getachew

Editor: Jennifer Kasoff
Editorial Production: Linda K. Schmidt
Production/Manufacturing: C.R. Bloodgood, Robert B. Shields
Maps: David Lindroth, Inc.

ESCAPE TO MOROCCO

Most books on the travel shelves are either long on the nitty-gritty and short on evocative photographs, or the other way around. We at Fodor's think that the different balance in this slim volume is just perfect, rather like the intersection of the most luscious magazine article and a sensible, down-to-earth guidebook. On the road, the useful pages at the end of the book are practically all you need. For the planning, roam through the color photographs up front: Each one reveals a key facet of the corner of Morocco it portrays and, together with the lyrical accompanying text, conveys a sense of place that will take you there before you go. Each page opens up one of Morocco's exceptional experiences; each spread leads you to the quintessential places that highlight the spirit of the country at its purest.

Some of these are sure to beckon. You may yearn to sip mint tea in palm-dappled shade in tiled courtyards, bargain for carpets and slippers in cacophonous souks, or discover mud castles, untouched mountain villages, blue-and-white towns, marvelous beaches, or pristine ancient ruins. You may consider journeying to the Tangier of Bowles and Bertolucci or to Marrakesh or the northernmost shore of Africa. You may seek

adventure: Experience a sandstorm in an oasis, watch the sun rise over a perfect dune, or take a twisting, turning drive along a precipitous road from the heights of the High Atlas all the way to the valley below. You may find shelter in a sultan's palace or end your day studying the million stars above the Sahara.

Author Pamela Windo discovered Morocco in 1989. The following year she went there again to live, write, and generally get away from it all. Hearing nothing from his mother, Windo's son, photographer Simon Russell, went in search of her and discovered the reason for her disappearance: The palms, the vaulted azure sky, the sandy kasbahs, and the snow-white peaks had conspired to beguile her.

It has happened to centuries of travelers before her, and it will happen to you. So be prepared to be bewitched by this exotic Land of the Setting Sun. Forget your projects and deadlines. And escape to Morocco. You owe it to yourself.

—The Editors

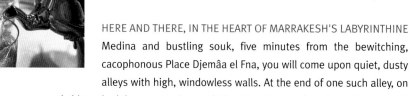

HERE AND THERE, IN THE HEART OF MARRAKESH'S LABYRINTHINE Medina and bustling souk, five minutes from the bewitching, cacophonous Place Djemâa el Fna, you will come upon quiet, dusty alleys with high, windowless walls. At the end of one such alley, on an unremarkable arched doorway, a sign reads RIAD ENIJA, in a perfect show of Marrakesh modesty: Hide what is precious. And so it is that riads, the trophy mansions of the old Moroccan bourgeoisie, are always plain and bare without and, within, sensual and refined beyond imagining. Two centuries ago, in Riad Enija, a wealthy silk merchant reclined on brocade cushions in a leafy courtyard where a fountain gurgled with water piped from the Atlas Mountains; he snapped his fingers at maids and cooks in ornate salons with high, richly painted cedar ceilings, multihued mosaic walls and tile floors, and curlicued window

Riad Enija

MOROCCAN STYLE, MARRAKESH

Your host at Riad Enija, Ursula, fulfills your every wish as if by magic, then discreetly leaves you to roam to your heart's content through her fairy-tale palace.

grilles. Today, the opulence inspires both an appetite for life and its contemplation. In your elegant bedroom, a silk-draped four-poster conjures exotic fantasies, and a low brass table set with fresh flowers bears luscious bowls of fruit and a pitcher of spring-water. Your bathroom is a vision, too, suffused with the perfume of white lilies, the walls shining like marble with their tadlak glaze. A bathrobe and velvet slippers are waiting to cosset you. Gilt tea glasses and a gleaming pot filled with mint tea sparkle in the sun. When the moon and evening stars rise above the courtyard and the heady aromas of cumin, coriander, and saffron drift into the night, you wander into the kitchen to watch Khadija, the riad's cook, prepare the evening meal. Dinner is served by candlelight on mosaic tables, with goblets of robust Moroccan cabernet and delicate tagines brimming with olives. Filled with hospitality, days here pass with rare timelessness, and it's easy to imagine being a Pasha, or a Pasha's wife, and like them, never leaving the riad.

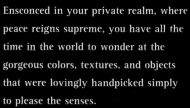

Ensconced in your private realm, where peace reigns supreme, you have all the time in the world to wonder at the gorgeous colors, textures, and objects that were lovingly handpicked simply to please the senses.

THE MYSTERIES OF THE VAST SAHARA UNFOLD SLOWLY AS YOU ARRIVE AT ITS EDGE. Two hours from Erfoud, at Auberge Ksar Sania, desert sparrows flutter in and out of the sunny reception room. Stay a night in one of its simple domed rooms. The next day, after the sun passes its blistering zenith, your camel caravan sets off on an hour-long trek. On a flat tract beneath soaring dunes, a campfire is set with brushwood and a shaggy-brown wool *fibule*, a nomad's traveling house, is staked down. Inside, comrades in adventure settle in to exchange stories over spicy couscous and wait for that magic moment when the red sun sets in the west and the sky turns purple-pink, then moonlit midnight blue, asparkle with stars. The fire dances in the breeze, the gas lanterns flicker, and strong mint tea warms you and perfumes the clear dry air. Blankets are passed around, and soon the camp is filled with the desert's sublime darkness and

A Desert Day and Night

SUNRISE AND SUNSET IN THE MERZOUGAN DUNES, THE SAHARA

Setting down in the twilight, your desert fantasy is fulfilled: You are far, far away from it all, enfolded in serenity and the hospitality of your desert friends.

silence. In the cool before dawn, you sit astride your camel to trek across the sculpted sands to the highest dune nearby, Erg Chebbi, to watch the sun rise. The climb to the summit is too steep for the camels, and it's a strenuous short hike. Your reward: a once-in-a-lifetime moment. Over the far-off Algerian horizon, after a first pale glow, the orange sun rises brilliantly and begins its journey west again. Everything about the desert trip is a challenge: the heat, the climb, the sand itself. Now, with mirages hovering in every direction, you blaze back to Erfoud in your Land Rover—more knowledgeable about the ways of the desert and carrying a bittersweet nostalgia for the Sahara, so harsh yet so very beautiful.

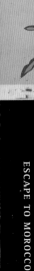

An ocean of sensual
curves undulates to the
distant horizon. The
gifts of the desert are
space, silence, and a
great sense of solitude.

Desert men have the desert's wisdom in their eyes. Camel driver El Hussain knows the great dune Erg Chebbi like his own back garden, and values his hardy desert transportation.

AN ARCHED MOORISH DOORWAY ON THE EXTREME northwestern tip of Africa at Cap Spartel leads you to the terra-cotta tile terrace at Le Mirage. Pristine white balustrades separate you from the endless aquamarine ocean and a cloudless azure sky. Like a siren, the blissful vision draws you into tranquil days of lazing in a deck chair beside a pool in a flower-filled garden. The view extends to infinity, embracing a wild, silver-sand beach that winds down the coast of Africa. In the distance, giant ships sail out through the Straits of Gibraltar into the vast Atlantic, bound for the Canaries and South America, finally just specks on the horizon. High above, a small biplane drones. Down below, heaving to and fro in the swell, fishing

Le Mirage

CAP SPARTEL, THE NORTHERN TIP OF AFRICA, THE MEDITERRANEAN COAST

The endless glistening ocean entices the imagination to soar like a bird, over the waves that converge from every direction on the cloudless horizon.

boats spread their nets in a snaking line. You may share the panorama with celebrity visitors to Le Mirage and weary foreign ambassadors who come up from Rabat to escape the cares of diplomacy. When the aroma of seafood interrupts your own reveries, head for the airy, elegant restaurant, which offers tender swordfish or marinated anchovies with chilled white wine as well as the ineffable mood and the endlessly beguiling views. As the afternoon light fades and the golden sun sinks into the west, the tawny Cap Spartel lighthouse, on its ocean-view ledge on the corner of Africa, beckons to weary seafarers bound for the port of Tangier. Sleep comes to you in your cozy, cliff-side chalet—so soft, sensual, and white—accompanied by the hushed whisper of waves on the shore.

STANDING HERE, INSIDE A KASBAH'S THICK CLAY-WALLED TURRET, IT SEEMS AS IF the earth itself has risen up to protect you. Great studded wooden doors with giant keyholes barricade the kasbah, but a local guide has taken you inside. Enter into earth-floored quadrants and walk through low arches, past hay-filled animal enclosures, up narrow, uneven, dusty, dark stairs to ruined aeries, and then out onto the turret rooftops. The kasbah's architecture is pure defense. A primitive enclave of truncated towers and crenellated walls decorated with tribal motifs, the southern kasbahs are fabricated from sun-dried pisé bricks—mud, mashed palm trunk, rubble, and water, the only materials at hand. The honey-colored kasbahs that make up Aït Benhaddou dominate a steep rocky mount beside the pebbly river Ounil. This is as close to an *Arabian Nights* fantasy as you can get—so spellbinding, especially at sunrise and

Kasbah Country

THE LAND OF MUD CASTLES, THE SOUTH

Walking inside a kasbah is like being inside a massive gingerbread cake. The well-kept feudal secrets dissolve with the mud-brick walls that crumble with time and the elements.

sunset, that scenes of *Lawrence of Arabia* were shot here. Ford the river and enter Aït Benhaddou from the right, through its encircling mud walls, between orchards of almond trees. On either side of the steeply ascending maze of alleys are the family kasbahs, some crumbling, some still intact, that once made up the fiefdom of the Khalif Benhaddou, a royal delegate sent from Marrakesh to subdue the southern Berber tribes. Sturdy and impenetrable, a kasbah defends a family or a whole tribe. But it cannot ward off nature's onslaught. In time, like sand castles, kasbahs crumble, mainly from dryness, for rain rarely falls in this region. Then it's time to move on and build another. Nomads forever, people of the desert merely move, knowing that the only thing that is constant is change.

DIN AND *DOUNIA*—SACRED AND PROFANE—are the Muslim principles guiding Fez, the spiritual capital of Morocco. The streets and markets are profane. All that is inside the high walls of mosques, palaces, and homes is sacred, their courtyards open to the heavens and filled with fountains and trees as a reminder of nature and Allah's goodness. When you catch a fleeting glimpse of the faithful at their rituals, it is only through a doorway—the lustrous cedar door opening into the red-carpeted mausoleum of Moulay Idriss II, for instance, or the shaded entrance to the white-and-green Ablutions Courtyard of the great green-tiled Kairaouine Mosque. Even the briefest look into these holy places illuminates the taste for the beautiful and

Fez the Mysterious

THE INNER COURTYARDS, FEZ AND THE MIDDLE ATLAS

The refinements and rituals of Fez life can be glimpsed beyond the Kairaouine Mosque's open-arched doorways and the great studded doors of private homes. La Maison Bleue is a rare exception—its mysteries accessible to all.

the meditative that is innate in the people of Fez. To penetrate the mystery of the inner courtyard, walk through the sunlit Medersa Bou Inania, an ancient Koranic school, stroll around the immense, cypress-filled central and private inner courtyards of Dar Batha Palace, once the retreat of a harem and now a museum, or dine in the ornate Mnebhi Palace, a restaurant that was once home to a Moroccan minister of war. Weary from your wanderings, return to La Maison Bleue, the mansion of Sidi Mohammed el Abbadi, the illustrious 19th-century judge and astrologer. Recline on a sumptuous sofa while an attendant serves mint tea in the formal ceramic-tiled courtyard. In an upstairs library saturated with history and sepia light, browse through letters and books written in flowing Arabic calligraphy, translated for you by your host, the judge's grandson Mehdi, and share his passion for the refinement, learning, and serenity that make Fez so intriguing.

AS THE IMPERIAL CITY AWAKENS AND MUEZZINS—THOSE chosen to chant the call to prayer—cry out from every minaret, make your way to the northern hilltop, by the jagged ruins of the Merenid Tombs. Beneath you the ivory metropolis spreads out in a vast impenetrable honeycomb across the wide valley of the river Fez, sliding down into the valley's heart. Here, Moulay Idriss I and his son founded the first Arab dynasty in Morocco. Below is your hotel, the Palais Jamaï, set amid mauve-blossomed jacarandas in the perfumed Andalusian garden. A moment-by-moment journey of discovery awaits you outside its doors. Negotiate the narrow alleys of the ever-crumbling, ever-standing labyrinth of Fez el Bali (Fez the Ancient). Ladies in bright djellabas and men in hooded

Fez the Knowable

SIGHTS IN THE SOUK

A bewitching collection of age-old bazaars, the souks of Fez make up the ultimate marketplace. You can spend anything from a few riels to several thousand dirhams.

burnooses emerge from dark doorways in dark alleys, going about their modern lives in the 9th-century citadel. Merchants and peddlers bustle around you, calling out *balek,* "watch yourself," as their heavily burdened mules miss you by a hair's breadth. Children play at your feet, oblivious of your passage. Around every sharp turn, another souk appears: the brass souk, the slipper souk, the embroidery, leather, and carpet souks. They offer anything you wish for. Watch as men sit over tea, poker-faced, playing the game of prices. The lowest price goes to the day's first customer, who brings good luck, and to the last. In between, what you pay depends on the strength of your desire, the rigor of your bargaining, the thickness of your pocketbook. Nothing in Morocco is what it seems. Everything is mirage, mystery, and sleight of hand.

At dawn and dusk, from the ruined tombs of the refined Merenids, the city of Fez spreads itself out before you in a panorama that has barely changed in a thousand years.

SET OUT FROM MARRAKESH AT DAWN ON THE STRAIGHT EUCALYPTUS-LINED ROAD that leads into the mighty snowcapped High Atlas far ahead. Olive trees quiver in the breeze, pine and juniper thicken on the rising mountainsides. Meander on, like the River Nfiss below, through the mud-made villages of Ouirgane, Ijoukak, and Imidl. The villages are beginning to stir: Smoke curls from a fire, a cockerel crows, children start off to school. This is the country of the Berber tribes who once controlled the mountain passes. High up to the left, with Mount Igdet behind it, is Agadir N'Gouj, the fortress-granary of the once-powerful Goundafi tribe. On the right, across the river, the rose-colored 12th-century Tin Mal Mosque soon appears, austere and roofless, the only mosque in Morocco that non-Muslims may enter. The landscape turns arid as the road climbs to the clouds blanketing 7,000-foot Tizi-n-Test pass. Suddenly, an

Over the Top

DRIVING THROUGH THE TIZI-N-TEST, THE HIGH ATLAS

The High Atlas are snowcapped until spring. Their fertile green valleys are filled with groves of walnut, olive, and almond trees, and with reminders of Berber dominance like the Tin Mal Mosque.

astonishing panorama opens up. Braced by the crisp high air, navigate the narrow road that loops down to the plain, 5,300 dizzying feet below. Limestone ridges swirl into red-earth valleys, where the low-lying green settlements soak up the last of the snowmelt. Surrounded by towering summits, hamlets cling to the slopes. To the south, gnarled argan trees speckle a vista of arid plains. In the valley the road flattens and runs along sandy expanses, mud-walled enclaves, and dry riverbeds. The desert is not far away. Head toward Taroudant between vast orange groves. Just when it seems the road will never end, the town's high ramparts appear. An archway leads you into the cool Hôtel Palais Salaam, its villas scattered around courtyards lush with fountains and banana palms. When you dive into the rippling turquoise pool, the distant mountains are briefly forgotten.

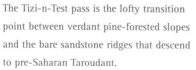

The Tizi-n-Test pass is the lofty transition point between verdant pine-forested slopes and the bare sandstone ridges that descend to pre-Saharan Taroudant.

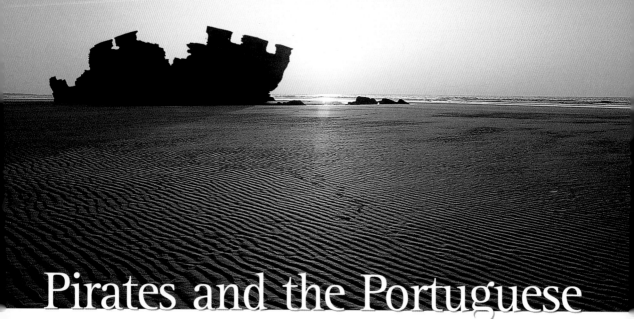

Pirates and the Portuguese

ESSAOUIRA, THE ATLANTIC COAST

SIT ON THE SEA SIDE OF THE THICK RAMPARTS, ABOVE THE VERDIGRIS CANNONS STILL POINTING OUT to sea, and look past the lichen-covered rocks and the swirling sea spray. You may think you see the shapes of pirate ships and Portuguese men-of-war off Essaouira's coast. Even today in this calm village you can easily imagine the battles that once raged along this part of the Barbary Coast, when the intrepid Portuguese were seizing seaports from Tangier to Agadir. Conquered successively by the Carthaginians, Romans, Portuguese, and Spanish and constantly marauded by pirate fleets, Morocco's coastline was a perilous place until the 18th century. Today, Essaouira is an unhurried fishing town, its crisscrossing alleys filled with houses painted blue, white, and yellow. Artisans carve auburn-hued thuya wood, hippies hang out in unpretentious cafés, seagulls soar over the day's catch of sardines heaped on the quay. It's hard to conceive of trouble and strife here. But up on the Sqala, one of the two sea bastions built by the warring Portuguese to protect their conquest, a sense of menace lingers. Chalk

up your fantasies of piracy and pillage to the rolling mist and the gulls' plaintive calls. But the phantoms fade with the sun, and after a walk on the long, glistening beach, you repair to a charming salon or a monastic-style dining room for the evening meal at Villa Maroc. Candles flicker in the iron candelabras above a rough stone arch; a steaming *tagine* arrives with an icy bottle of Gris de Boulâouane rosé. Time to toast the pleasures of peace.

Miles down the beach, a chunk of Carthaginian ruin like an ancient shipwreck entices beach walkers. In the port, choose your fish and take a seat at an umbrella-shaded communal table. Your main course will be grilled before your eyes.

THE SCENT OF ROSES IS SIGN ENOUGH THAT YOU HAVE ARRIVED in El Kelâa M'Gouna in April or May. The perfume hangs heavy over the thick, green rose hedges crowding the roadside. Brightly bescarved ladies pick the full, velvety flowers and mound them in large squares of black lace or raffia bags. For reasons long since forgotten, the damask rose was brought here from France in 1938 by one Monsieur de Bigouane; it was he who opened the town's famous Capp Florale rose-water distillery. El Kelâa M'Gouna has celebrated the yearly harvest of the pink roses ever since. The excitement is pervasive. Girls and boys wear rose garlands, and street stalls sell soaps, scents, and dried buds. Knock at the distillery door and ask for the manager—a friendly request may yield a tour. Inside, deep, fragrant carpets of pink roses fill whole sheds, where bamboo

Ode to a Rose

THE MOUSSEM OF EL KELÂA M'GOUNA, THE SOUTH

The spring harvest of the lovely damask rose is celebrated every year with full-blown folklore festivities, with dancing, drums, and haunting tribal chants.

canopies gently filter the sunlight, creating a surreal vision of heavenly pink. If this sight isn't enough, elbow through the intense throngs in the town arena. Your goal: the stand reserved for foreign visitors and other dignitaries, with the best view of the festivities. On red carpets, a bevy of women in pink organza and tulle and white-turbaned, white-robed men, from different Berber tribes and different regions, pour into the arena, all intoning raw, powerful desert chants and pounding thick-skinned drums as they sway in unison and loop in shifting circles. Finally, Miss Rose is crowned, a dark-eyed beauty with an elaborate, high-piled hair arrangement, silver necklaces, and a black–sequined robe decorated with bright tassels. In hot, dry, dusty El Kelâa M'Gouna, the delicate rose seems an anomaly. Back at the quiet Auberge Rosa Damaskina, on a riverbank outside town, sip chilled rosé over dinner with a night view of kasbahs and the silhouettes of palm trees under a star-filled sky—the carpets of blossoms still vividly rosy in your memory.

Thanks to the toil of a solitary Frenchman in the 1940s, visions of pink roses, singly on the bush, and en masse in the distillery, fill the dusty southern settlement of El Kelâa M'Gouna and the surrounding pre-Saharan landscape. The flowers' petals and perfume are fleeting, but their beauty will last forever in your memory.

Pearl of the South

PALACES, COURTYARDS AND GARDENS, MARRAKESH

AFRICA MEETS ARABIA IN THE VIBRANT, INTOXICATING, RED-EARTH OASIS CITY OF MARRAKESH—THE Pearl of the South, Jewel of the South, The Rose City. Every sultan of every dynasty has coveted and rebuilt this strategic center for caravan traders. Inebriated by the dry, clear air and charmed by the rivers flowing from the mountains, they built palaces, courtyards, and gardens meant for religious contemplation and sensual pleasure. Dramatic contrasts leap out at every turn: blazing sunlight and dark shadows, sandy soil and lush foliage, refined, mosaic-encrusted columns and rough pisé walls, Gnaouan rhythms and Andalusian melodies, flat fertile plains and, behind them, snowcapped High Atlas peaks. When you are inside the thick, towering ramparts, in the heart of the medieval Medina, everything is dusty and salmon-pink. But step inside the Palais el Bahiaóthe, loveliest of Marrakesh's palaces, where Ben Kinsgley starred in the movie *Harem*, and you will experience one of the greatest contrasts of all. Built for the harem of the Vizir Bou Ahmed, it is lavish and serene. Faience columns and stucco cornices are inscribed with Koranic

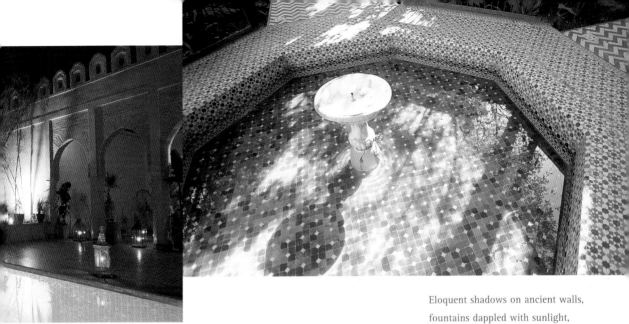

Eloquent shadows on ancient walls, fountains dappled with sunlight, a sense of beauty as old as the mountains—these are the things to savor in Marrakesh.

verses and intertwining leaves, and marble fountains stand in courtyards beside profuse gardens perfumed by orange blossoms and jasmine. "Court within court," wrote an enchanted Edith Wharton from the favorite wife's chambers during her 1917 visit. Nearby are the haunting, bijou Dar Si Said and the magnificent ruined Palais El Bodi, with its lagoon and sunken gardens. And at the end of the day, make your winding way via canopied, horse-drawn calèche to the pavilion and lagoon of La Menara, set in a vast, royal olive grove. It's a pleasurable place to pause before you negotiate the rough, narrow alleys through the Medina to the Scheherazadian restaurant El Yacout, where fragrant rose petals are scattered on your table, by a lapis pool, and waiters in monastic white djellabas deftly make you, too, feel like a sultan in his palace.

BARELY TOUCHED BY TIME AND RARELY VISITED, AÏT BOU GMEZ is made for the hiker and naturalist. The River Lakhdar snakes a clear path through the wide, emerald-green valley, an alluvial plain stretching for about 15 miles at 6,000 feet, hidden deep in the High Atlas. Roam through the mud-house hamlets on foot. You'll see farmers bearing huge handmade plows like crosses on their shoulders, striding across miniature brown fields bordered by great walnut trees. The tingling early morning silence is broken only by birdsong, swishing water, and the children's voices echoing from each village. For a giant's view, climb the strange, unmistakable conical mount in the middle of the valley to the *agadir,* a ruined fortress that once stored the villagers' grain. Or hire an expert Berber guide to lead a trek through a rugged mountain pass. The region is full of giant

The Descendants of Gmez

THE GREEN VALLEY OF AÏT BOU GMEZ, THE HIGH ATLAS

Surrounded on all sides by the silent peaks of the High Atlas, the valley of Aït Bou Gmez has so far escaped the ever-advancing tide of tourism.

crests, yawning caves filled with delicate white asphodels, and honeycomb settlements emerging from strategic outcrops. In spring there's a bite to the air—it might even snow. But in your midvalley accommodations, mud-walled, thatched-roofed Dar Itrane—House of the Stars in Berber—a blazing log fire and a spicy lamb *tagine* warm each evening. Candles light the convivial scene, and you and your fellow guests share bottles of hearty red wine. At night, peace and darkness reign. Breakfast on the sun-drenched terrace is a celebration of nature with its startling view of towering mountain peaks topped by the bluest of cornflower-blue skies and of pine-covered slopes reaching down to green fields. More restful, even, than the astounding panorama: as far as the eye can see, there's not a single sign of modern civilization.

In a house that
seems like all the rest,
Dar Itrane is spartan
with a touch of rustic
elegance. Meals of
country fare take second
place to the scenery.

SUNSET IS THE SIGNAL FOR THE WORLD'S MOST exotic carnival to begin in Djemâa el Fna. The morning square is fresh and clean. By midday cacophony reigns. By evening pleasure-hunters are streaming in boisterous waves through the surrounding souks, toward the Djemâa. Head for the topmost terrace of the Café de France or Café Argana and sip hot mint tea, as the sunset sky turns golden pink, orange, mauve, and scarlet. Gas lamps and braziers glow at outdoor food stalls as gaudy day turns to scintillating night. At the far end of the square, the towering Koutoubia Mosque stands sentinel, a sober stone reminder of order and of Islam. Descend from your safe terrace vantage point to join the shifting throng of human

Carnival Supreme

DJEMÂA EL FNA, MARRAKESH

Day and night, crowds jam the marketplace. Not so long ago here, criminals' severed heads were displayed on stakes to warn the wicked.

forms, among amusements and refreshments of every kind. All sense of direction, of time and place, and of everything ordinary and familiar disappears amid the raucous chants of cobra charmers, the antics of raving storytellers, the hypnotic cymbals of Gnaoua musician-exorcists singing in Arabic to African rhythms, and the beguiling entreaties of veiled ladies with kohl-lined eyes peddling amulets to ward off the evil eye. Reality lies outside this magic circle, and there—beyond the soothsayers with their tarotlike cards and past the tooth-pullers' stalls with their mounds of molars that set your own teeth on edge—are the calèches and taxis waiting to escort you safely home.

Set out on eye-catching stalls
in Djemâa el Fna are exotic
dishes such as steamed sheep's
head, stuffed spleen, spiced
snails, and harira soup. As
your digestif, watch families
of acrobats build human
pyramids and fly through
the air.

For Marrakshis, life in the Djemâa el Fna revolves around its cafés and souks. Every commodity and artifact under the sun can be found here, from green, pink, and black olives to kilims, rugs, slippers, and fairy-tale lanterns.

IN THE LABYRINTHINE SOUKS OF MARRAKESH AND IN ALL the souks of Morocco, among the myriad pyramids of rainbow-colored spices, are baskets of dried green leaves and lime-green powder—henna, bringer of beauty, plant of paradise and love. The leaves are ground, the powder mixed with water and sometimes tea or lemon juice to create a paste that dyes the skin red; the greener the powder, it is said, the stronger the effect. Here in Morocco, the sight of hands covered up to the wrists with intricate patterns in dark brick-red, sometimes almost black, and feet covered from sole to ankle, is as common as nail polish or makeup in other countries. A sensual bodily beautification for brides, henna is said to attract *baraka*—good luck—to a marriage, inspiring desire in husbands' eyes. In Djemâa el Fna, veiled henna ladies approach you

For the Love of Henna

A SENSUAL ART, MARRAKESH

Henna has a multitude of meanings: it's a message to Eros, a welcome pleasure for the eyes, and a coded sign of identity, of belonging to a tribe.

with pattern books. You can spend 15 minutes having a bracelet or anklet applied, or a motif that seductively curls down your ring finger, or three hours on designs that completely cover your hands and feet. Each henna artist designs according to her tribe and her own inspiration—always the same theme but always different in the details. In the north of Morocco, the designs are fluid and elaborate, the intertwining leaves of Islamic art. In the south, they're bold, pagan, and geometric. Whatever you choose, it's a labor of love, for the paste must stay on all night to produce the deepest color. Carefully applied and devoutly cared for, your henna makes a voluptuous memento of your journey.

A NARROW RIBBON OF ROAD LEADS YOU THROUGH THE STARK Anti-Atlas into the remote Ameln Valley. There, encircled by rose-hued, razor-edged ridges, the tranquil green valley is dotted with sandy-pink villages cleaving to the mountain slopes or resting at their feet as if sculpted from the granite. At the valley's center lies Tafraoute, your base camp, a quaint town with wilderness at its edges. From here, explore the villages—Oumesnat, Anameur, Adaï—where a quixotic contrast of tranquillity and turmoil prevails. Each quiet hamlet emerges uncannily from giant pink boulders heaped in mad disarray. One piled on top of another, the pink giants defy gravity, as if frozen in time after some tumultuous explosion. Where the stones came to rest, the ingenious Berbers built their homes, balancing on them, daringly using them as walls,

The Pink Wild West

TAFRAOUTE AND THE AMELN VALLEY, THE ANTI-ATLAS

Like heralds of spring, clouds of pink and white almond blossom decorate the winter-stark trees in and around the hidden villages of the Ameln Valley.

foundations, and sheltering archways. Pink mountains, pink boulders, pink homes. Chaos became order. Stroll through the hushed hamlets where vegetable gardens are tended by women and girls covered from head to toe by shiny, black-sequined robes. From a distance, in groups on the road, they call out to you brazenly. Face to face, they are like shy gazelles. Smiles, *bonjours*, and a *salaam w'aleykum* work wonders, though. That's often all it takes for them to invite you into their homes for tea. After your explorations, walk back to Tafraoute and up to the pool terrace of Hôtel les Amandiers. Perched above the town on a mountain of boulders, the hotel is named after the surrounding almond trees, which bloom in a flurry of pink and white in early spring. Pull up a chaise longue and watch as the sun gently sets and shafts of sunlight play between the endless peaks, dyeing them salmon-pink and golden rose.

In a landscape like a long-gone giant's playground, ancient argan trees, their gnarled trunks like writhing alligators, spring up miraculously among the eerie forms of the boulders, fissures, and chasms, and on the mountain slopes of the otherwise barren Anti-Atlas. Their oil is legendary and much sought after— nutty, light, and wholesome.

LEAVING RESTFUL ESSAOUIRA BEHIND, DRIVE NORTHWARD, hugging the rugged, deserted coastline once so prized by the Portuguese. Their sea bastions still stand on the beautiful Atlantic shores, all the way from Agadir to Asilah. Along the coast road, sudden bends reveal sheer cliff faces and steep drops to sandy coves where the translucent ocean ripples in. In Souira Kedima, a white-domed *marabout*—the mausoleum of a local holy man—stands at the sea's edge, washed by the surf. Continue on to Safi, where the Portuguese built their imperious, gray-stone Sea Castle, silent and well-preserved in its old age. Farther north are the surprises of Oualidia: a wild, dazzling seascape, a perfect blue lagoon, oyster beds, spider crabs, and a sleepy yesteryear charm. Savor mouthwatering seafood overlooking the lagoon

Beaches and Sea Bastions

A SEASIDE DRIVE, THE ATLANTIC COAST

Beyond the dunes at Diabat is Auberge Tangaro, a delicious base for strolls along the miles of sandy beaches.

in the Restaurant l'Arraignée's shady pergola. Then while away the afternoon in a blue rowboat, skimming around the sandbanks; or walk to the rock pools on the beach where fishermen bring in their bountiful catch of spider crabs. From Oualidia on up the coast for miles, the shimmering Atlantic is edged with patchwork parcels of land sewn with crops moistened by sea mist. Back on the road, the white city of El Jadida appears ahead, sprawling around a white-sand bay, pulling you onward: those Portuguese again, and the signs of their long dominance of Morocco's coastline. Here, in their most impressive conquest, is the subterranean Cistern. The reflection of the 25 slender-arched columns in the water teases your sense of perspective. Outside, walk along the sea bastion and around the ramparts overlooking the fishing port. Then check in at the Moorish, meditative Hôtel Palais Andalous, away from El Jadida's bay, and rest from the relentless sun and sea breezes.

Between Essaouira and Safi, the cliffs drop down to quiet beaches and coves. At Souira Kedima, the white-domed resting place of a local holy man lies at the Atlantic's edge, lapped by turquoise waves.

The subterranean Cistern of El Jadida is a reminder that the Portuguese were masters of architecture as well as of naval conquests. Oualidia was left in peace to enjoy the tides of its blue lagoon and the abundant catch of spider crabs.

YOU WALK WHERE ROMAN FEET ONCE WALKED, AMONG TALL grasses and bloodred geraniums, beside the bleached mosaic floors of the ruins of Volubilis, one of Rome's most distant conquests, long unprotected but miraculously preserved. From the steep twin hills of Moulay Idriss, the ruins are visible first as a series of columns accompanied by a line of cypresses. Then arches and walls come into focus, scattered across a slope above a great green plateau that stretches to the horizon and is dominated by a triumphal arch. Now inhabited only by lazy storks who nest in the column tops, the ruins are drowsy and unkempt; much remains unexcavated. Cross the thin Fertassa River and ramble among the marble columns and through the weedy Basilica. Explore the House of Orpheus and the Temple of Saturn, and

The Romans Remain

VOLUBILIS, FEZ, AND THE MIDDLE ATLAS

Volubilis's view of Roman ruins and an ancient plateau is transfixing. It was used by Martin Scorcese as a backdrop for his film The Last Temptation of Christ.

sit beside the regal columns of the Capitol. Walking in ancient footsteps is a heady experience, but the history of the place keeps you rooted to the ground. This is the ancient gathering place of civilizations: Berber, Roman, and Arab. Once regional capital of the Berber kingdom of Mauritania, Volubilis was annexed by Claudius in AD 45. The Romans cultivated olives on the slopes and grain on the plains and even supplied lions for the Roman games. When the Roman Empire fell, the Berbers reappropriated their capital, living alongside Jewish, Greek, and Syrian immigrants until a rapacious 17th-century sultan, Moulay Ismail, stripped Volubilis of its treasures to enhance his capital, the nearby city of Meknes. Your exploration complete, walk up to the solitary Volubilis Inn. At dinner on a vine-covered terrace, surrounded by pomegranates and jasmine, devour your last view of the noble ruins before they disappear into the darkness.

SOMETHING WHERE THERE IS NOTHING, *OUAHA*—THIS IS THE meaning of oasis. The earth gives forth, man cultivates: figs, olives, pomegranates, and apricots, the fruits of the Garden of Eden. But in the oasis, date palms rule, their waving fronds beckoning you into a refuge of coolness and plump berries. The barren, velvety-gray Kissane Mountains run parallel to the wide green River Drâa, which flows for a thousand miles in the scorching rocky *hamada,* or desert, across to Cap Drâa on the Atlantic Ocean, sustaining myriad oasis gardens sheltered by a million date palms. The road into the oasis town of Zagora is dusty; the desert is close. Over the bridge, beneath Mount Zagora, the hotel La Fibule du Drâa's archway leads into an oasis within the oasis. The owner beams in welcome and shakes your hand. All is cool, calm.

A Date in the Oasis

ZAGORA, THE SOUTH

The branches of the date palm—*phoenix dactylfera*—burn red at harvest time. The legend of the phoenix was inspired by the sight of birds rising from these flaming branches.

Towering palms shade the aquamarine pool; the Koran says all trees must be built around, never cut down. If you swim at midnight under the star-filled sky, the only sounds are swishing palm fronds and the chatter of roosting birds. The next day begins like a dream: sunshine, fresh air, cloudless blue sky. Then one of Zagora's mild sandstorms blows into town. Never mind. Ignoring the swirling sand, explore the walled enclave of Ksar Tissergate and the gardens beyond, where forests of date palms drip with brown berries on flame-red branches, and life goes on. The short wheat is emerald green, men till and tend their plots, boys ride by on donkeys, and women wash clothes in water channels while their children play hide-and-seek. No one asks why you are there, or where you are going. The oasis is Allah's garden.

The oasis can be a sun-filled secret garden one moment and a jungle of sand-veiled silhouettes the next. The people of the desert know this, and are curious to know you, too.

Paradise Valley

LAND OF THE IDA OUTANANE, HOTEL DES CASCADES, THE HIGH ATLAS

TUCKED AWAY AT THE WESTERN EXTREMITY OF THE HIGH ATLAS CHAIN, WHERE IT MEETS THE Atlantic Ocean, is the gorgeous Paradise Valley and at its heart the Cascades d'Immouzer des Ida Outanane, a series of powerful waterfalls, and the idyllic Hotel des Cascades. Both are known to only a few connoisseurs. Getting there is one-half the pleasure, as the British hikers must have learned when they discovered the valley in the 1960s. The winding, tortuous road follows a glinting stream carved into a yellow sandstone gorge edged with pink oleanders. Perfumed by wild lavender and thyme, carpeted with yellow gorse, and wooded with pine, carob, olive, and almond trees, the valley is the habitat of white doves and cuckoos, skylarks and partridge, even eagles. As the road climbs higher, the narrow valley deepens, and the towering, glistening palm trees thicken. Golden wheat grows here and there on narrow plateaus; gingerbread hamlets hang brazenly over precipices. In spring, the falls are visible from the road as they plunge between the dense vegetation. In dry

Ride out on a mule at dawn's first light to explore the lavender-filled valley. When you return, the shady arbors of the Hotel des Cascades are the perfect respite from midday heat.

months, only a trickle drizzles down into the falls' deep aquamarine pools, where local boys entertain tourists who have ventured this far with hair-raising dives from the overhanging rocks. A sign near the cascades points to the hotel, which perches on a slope above the falls. Stand and get your bearings on its wide sandstone terrace, which overlooks the valley you just came through; the ocean is just visible on the far-off horizon, a faint line. Later, wander through gardens ablaze with roses, geraniums, and calendula and seek refuge in shady bowers of jasmine, fig, and mulberry. At dusk, sip a cocktail to the rustling of poplars and the gurgling of springs on their way down the mountains.

GREEK LEGEND RECOUNTS HOW HERCULES SLEW THE GIANT ANTAEUS AND FATHERED a son by his widow, Tingé; in her honor, the stories tell us, the son founded a city that blessed her name. This is the old capital of the Roman province Mauritania Tingitania. Tangier, as it has since been known, has seen every seafaring nation of the world come and go through the Straits of Gibraltar. In the 1920s, the city's heyday, it became the favored tax-free hideaway of wealthy expats and the favorite muse of writers, painters, and dreamers. All were searching to escape their particular ennui, and all were taken hostage by the city's potpourri of charms, its cloudless skies, its sea air, its splendid light. Tangier's biggest fan, Paul Bowles, once described it as "a great pile of child's building blocks strewn carelessly over the hillside." In the Grand and Petit Socco markets, the artists sat—and still sit—in smoke-filled cafés, watching the exotic

City of Dreams

TANGIER, THE MEDITERRANEAN COAST

Lapped by two great seas, the ancient city of Tangier is kept alive by legends and ghosts: fearless seafarers, audacious artists, and those in pursuit of their own private dreams.

commotion and listening to the wail of Moorish music and the din of the souks. On Rue d'Angleterre, the broken green window in the abandoned Gran Hôtel Villa de France was Matisse's private viewpoint. From there, captivated by the supernatural light, as was Delacroix before him, he conjured his *Fenêtre à Tangier*. Bowles soaked up the glorious view from the Café Hafa and felt at home in the faded Hotel Continental, appearing there for a brief moment in Bernardo Bertolucci's rendering of *The Sheltering Sky*. These days the city has gone to seed. Its treasures lie beneath weeds or behind ruined walls. But its spirit lives on. And from a sea-view balcony at the Hotel El Minzah, you may also find yourself entranced by the potent potion of light, color, and knowing world-weariness that gives this city of dreams its eternal allure.

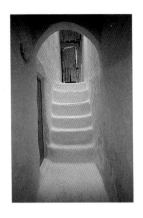

DEEP IN RIF COUNTRY, CLOUD-ENSHROUDED TWIN PEAKS LOOM HIGH ABOVE A mountain village. At the top of Chefchaouen, inside steeply sloping ramparts, cobbled alleys course downward from a medieval square. In these zigzagging alleys you are plunged into a thalassic world where every curve and arch, every door and window is washed with ice-blue paint and splashed with cobalt, turquoise, and other brazen blues. Dreamlike and hallucinatory, the bends, the arcades, the disappearing stone steps, and the sudden cul-de-sacs draw you onward in search of the source of these bold colors. Inside enticing, half-open doorways, white and ice-blue flow over walls and floors. At once cool and exuberant, the color makes a sharp contrast to the town's somber fortifications, chills summer's inferno, enlivens winter's gloom, and calms religious fervor. The descendants of Muslim refugees who painted this holy town had

Ice-Blue and Isolated

CHEFCHAOUEN, THE RIF MOUNTAINS

Follow the streets from Plaza Uta el Hammam along electrifying sky-blue walls crowding perfectly painted ice-blue steps and through arresting, steeply slanting aquamarine alleys.

fled here from Andalusia; the blue gave them courage and reminded them of home. Once upon a time, during the 15th century, Chefchaouen was a base camp for local forces battling the invading Portuguese, and it was isolated from the outside world for many years afterward—its gates were closed to foreigners until the early 1900s. Today, only the Nikes under men's tented burnooses remind you of this century. Custom and respect for tradition remain deep-rooted. Wander at will and stay at Casa Hassan, a discreet and peaceful inn near Plaza Uta el Hammam that was the proprietor's birthplace. From its tea terrace, all of Chefchaouen and its surrounding peaks unfurl before you. You are at once away from it all and at home in this friendly village, where everyone still greets you with a Spanish *hola*.

Early morning sunshine
bathes the white houses
near Place el Makhzen
in Chefchaouen, casting
stark shadows here
and there amid the
seaside hues of
the mountain citadel.

All the Details

Royal Air Maroc (tel. 800/344–6726) operates the only direct service between North America and Morocco, with several weekly 6½-hour flights from New York's JFK airport to Casablanca. There are daily connections to Marrakesh, Agadir, Tangier, Fez, and Ouarzazate. TWA has a code-share with RAM for some flights.

Fax and telephone are more reliable than mail for making hotel reservations. From the United States, dial the international access code, 011, plus Morocco's country code, 212, plus the local area code (minus its initial zero), plus the number. Properties are open year-round and most take credit cards unless noted otherwise. All prices in this book are quoted in Moroccan dirhams. At press time 9.92DH equals U.S.$1.

Good train lines serve Tangier, Rabat, Casablanca, Meknes, Fez, and Marrakesh, and a relay system of inexpensive communal taxis called *grands taxis* covers the whole country. International and local car-rental agencies are plentiful. Main roads are mostly two lanes, with uneven, sandy shoulders, and traffic can be fast.

Morocco enjoys year-round sunshine, but the best times to visit are April through June, September, and October. Midsummer is very hot, and winter weather is changeable.

Common sense will tell you how to dress and which magic carpets to buy at what price. Bargaining is a way of life in Morocco, not just a way to torture travelers, so give it a whirl and see what bargains you can garner. Moroccans are inordinately friendly and hospitable, so try saying *salam w'aleykum* (peace be with you) and *insh'allah* (if God is willing). When planning your trip, keep in mind that during the month of Ramadan, schedules change and service may be erratic. In 2000 and 2001, Ramadan begins late in November and lasts 29 or 30 days.

The Moroccan tourist board, ONMT, has offices in New York (tel. 212/557–2520, fax 212/949–8148), Fez (Place Mohammed V, tel. 05/62–47–69), and Marrakesh (Place Abdelmoumen, Gueliz, tel. 04/43–61–31 or 04/43–62–39, fax 04/65–43–70).

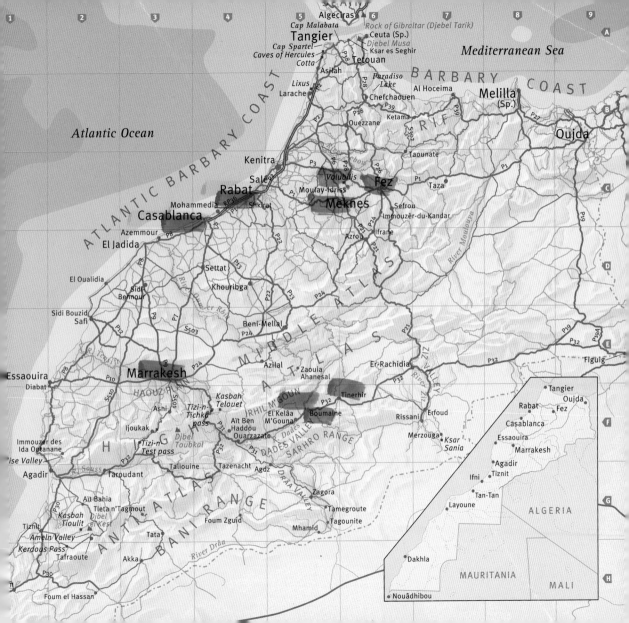

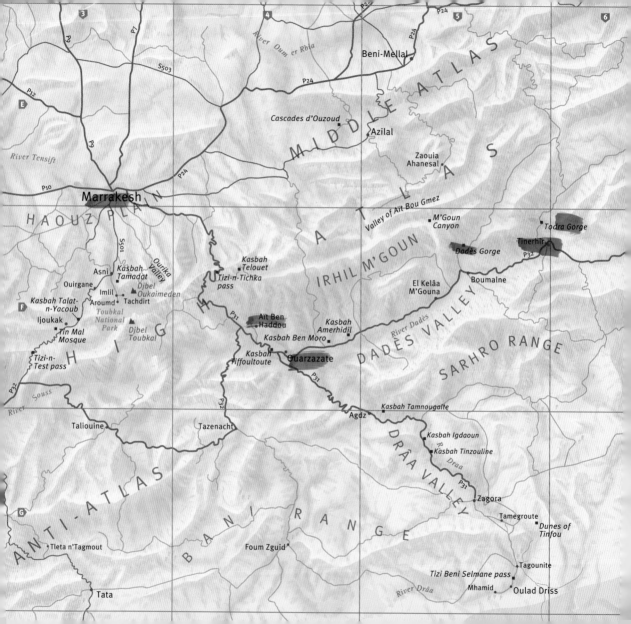

Grid coordinates, listed after town names in the following section, refer to the map on page 79 and to the detail map on page 80.

THE MEDITERRANEAN COAST

Morocco's coastline stretches 805 km (500 mi) along the Mediterranean. It is part of the Barbary Coast, which stretches from Tripoli around the tip of Africa and down the Atlantic. Along its shores sailed all the ancient sailors, from Phoenicians to Portuguese, scouting prosperous ports to colonize, as well as pirates, who plundered ships of every nation. The ancient Greeks imagined the Hesperides to be daughters of the sunset and their garden to lie at the extreme western limits of the Other World, beyond the river Oceanus, somewhere between Cap Spartel (5A) and the Roman ruins of Lixus near Larache (5B). Hercules completed his 11th labor in the garden, slaying the dragon Ladon and picking the golden apples while Atlas held up the pillars of the world—the Pillars of Hercules, Djebel Musa (6A), on African shores, and the Rock of Gibraltar, Djebel Tarik (6A), in Spain. The northern part of Morocco is much cooler than the south; the best time to visit is May through September.

TANGIER, CITY OF DREAMS (5A)

City of Dreams p. 72

Unlike other writers who flitted back and forth to Tangier for their inspiration, Paul Bowles lived most of his life here, almost single-handedly creating Tangier's mystique for the rest of the world. Apart from the Petit Socco cafés, favorite artist-and-writer haunts include Café Hafa, with its inspiring sea views, and Café Detroit, opened in the '60s by beat writer Brion Gysin. St. Andrew's Church is a surprising mix of English country church and Moorish mosque. London *Times* correspondent Walter Harris lies in its shaded, tree-filled graveyard with the epitaph: *He loved the Moorish people and was their friend*. The famous Hotel El Minzah once hosted the likes of Barbara Hutton and Douglas Fairbanks.

CONTACT Hotel El Minzah, 85 rue de la Liberté, 90000 Tangier, tel. 09/93−58−85, fax 09/93−45−46, elminzah@tangeroise.net.ma.

DISTANCES 363 km (225 mi) from Casablanca, 315 km (196 mi) from Fez.

FACILITIES 123 rooms, 17 suites with air-conditioning, phone, TV. 2 restaurants, piano bar, pool, garden café, 4 tennis courts, fitness center.

PRICES Double, high season (July−Aug.) 1,450DH−1,750DH. Double, low season (Jan.−May, Sept.−Dec.) 1,250DH−1,550DH. Prices vary with sea or street view. Suite 1,900DH−3,500DH. Royal suite 6,500DH−8,500DH, depending on season. Buffet breakfast 120DH, other meals 250DH.

OTHER OPTIONS The Hotel Continental: One of Tangier's oldest hostelries, opened in 1865, this place near the Petit Socco is faded but not without charm. Queen Victoria's son, Alfred, and painter Edgar Degas both stayed here. Dar Baroud 36, Tangier, tel. 09/93−10−24, fax 09/93−11−43. 55 rooms, 4 suites, some with balconies and sensational port views. Terrace café. Double 276DH, suite 750DH, including breakfast. **Villa Kharroubia:** This was the home of the late Honorable David Herbert, second son of the Earl of Pembroke, once known as the King of the Mountain. You can enjoy sea, city, and port views from the huge flower garden here. Jamâa el Mokrâa, Place du Cadi, Tangier, tel. 09/33−58−46, fax 09/93−47−57. 3 rooms, 1 single, all with bath. 2 terraces, small pool. Weekly rental for house 23,000DH−94,000DH, depending on number of guests and season. Meals 150DH−250DH.

CAP SPARTEL, THE NORTHERN TIP OF AFRICA (5A)

Le Mirage p. 18

The coastline around the northwestern tip of Africa is rugged and wooded. The road to Cap Spartel from Tangier goes over famous La Montagne, filled with foreign palaces and villas. The Cap Spartel lighthouse was erected by a multinational consortium after a disastrous shipwreck that drowned more than 250 Brazilian cadets. Le Mirage, 14 km (9 mi) west of

Tangier on an unspoiled, sparsely inhabited stretch of coast, is beside the Caves of Hercules (5A). The caves were inhabited in prehistoric times. There is an eye-catching rock chasm opening onto the ocean. From here a rough path leads about 1¼ km (½ mi) to Cotta (5A), the 2nd- to 3rd-century Roman settlement famed for producing anchovy paste.

CONTACT Ahmed and Abdeslam Chakkour, Le Mirage, Grottes d'Hercule, B.P. 2198 Tangier, tel. 09/93—33—32, fax 09/93—34—92, mirage@iam.net.ma.

DISTANCES 377 km (234 mi) from Casablanca, 329 km (204 mi) from Fez.

FACILITIES 22 luxury chalets with sea views and terraces. Restaurant, piano bar, room service, TV, phone, beach. Near Royal Golf Club.

PRICES Double, high season (July—mid-Sept.) 1,200DH; suite 1,800DH—2,900DH for 2–4 people. Double, low season (mid-Mar.—June, mid-Sept.—mid-Nov.) 960DH; suite 1,080DH—2,160DH for 2–4 people. Breakfast 80DH.

THE MEDITERRANEAN COAST HIGHLIGHTS
From Ksar es Seghir to Cap Malabata and across to Tangier there are magnificent savage cliffs and sandy coves where you can swim and camp to your heart's content. From Cap Spartel the view is of Spain's shores, the Mediterranean waves meeting the Atlantic, and a silver shoreline disappearing down the coast of Africa. Near Le Mirage and the Caves of Hercules there's a simple open-air café perched on the cliffside where you can eat fresh-grilled sardines while watching the sun set over the Atlantic.

THE RIF MOUNTAINS

The rugged Rif mountains reach across the northern shoulder of Africa from Tetouan (6A), around the Mediterranean coastline toward the Algerian border, and inland down to Taounate (6C) and Taza (7C). The rough market town of Ketama (7B) at the heart of the Rif

is the main point of sale for kif, or hashish, and, given the town's history of tourist harrassment, is best avoided. This said, the zigzagging road that runs through it from Fez to Chefchaouen lies smack on the high limestone backbone of the wild Rif ridges, a rugged landscape of vast lonely views and sparsely populated cedar, oak, and pine forests. The best time to visit is summer. Winter can be gray and rainy.

CHEFCHAOUEN (6B)
Ice-Blue and Isolated p. 74

Chefchaouen's flat cobbled Plaza Uta el Hammam is the coolest place in the village—and a favorite hangout of hippies in search of peace and a quiet joint—with friendly cafés in the shade of mulberry trees. Moulay Ismail's Kasbah, with its enclosed garden, lies at the top end of the plaza, next to the pink-stone Great Mosque. The town was built to honor the holy man Moulay Abdessalam ben Mchich, whose tomb in the nearby mountains makes the whole region sacred to Muslims. Behind the Chefchaouen peaks is Paradiso Lake, where local guide Said bin Ayad (contact him through the Hotel Parador; *see* Other Option, *below*) can take you over Allah's Natural Bridge, a rock formation, to swim and see the monkeys.

CONTACT Casa Hassan, 22 rue Targhui, Chefchaouen, tel. 09/98—61—53, fax 09/98—81—96.

DISTANCES 198 km (123 mi) from Fez, 219 km (136 mi) from Casablanca.

FACILITIES 6 rooms with 2 shared baths, 2 suites with shower and fireplace. Restaurant, rooftop café for guests.

PRICES Double 250DH, suite 450DH, including breakfast and dinner.

ANOTHER OPTION Hotel Parador: All the rooms here are basic and clean. There's a small pool with sensational mountain views. Place El Makhzen, Chefchaouen, tel. 09/98—63—24 or 09/98—61—36, fax 09/98—70—33. 21 rooms with bath and TV, 12 rooms with shower, 2 suites with bath, air-conditioning, and TV. Restaurant, bar. Double

516DH, suite 1,320DH, including breakfast. Other meals 80DH—150DH.

THE RIF MOUNTAINS HIGHLIGHTS

Medieval **Chefchaouen** (6B) is the most unusual and attractive of the Rif towns. Larger, white-washed **Tetouan** (6A), with its unique medina built by Jewish and Muslim refugees from Andalusia, began as the Mauretanian city Tamuda in 3 BC. It later became the 14th-century Merenids' base, from which they controlled the dissident Rifian tribes, and ended as the capital of the Spanish protectorate from 1912 to 1956. On the coast, the Rif ridges drop down to **Al Hoceima** (7B), a small, sprawling seaside resort with a turquoise bay that is crowded with Moroccan vacationers in midsummer but a haven of peace out of season.

FEZ AND THE MIDDLE ATLAS

The Middle Atlas lie about 100 km (62 mi) south of Fez, extending southwest from the Rif in the north to meet the High Atlas northeast of Marrakesh. Used as pasture by nomadic shepherds, they are thickly covered with oak and giant cedar and are snow-covered in winter. Sefrou (6C) is an old Berber stronghold surrounded by cherry orchards. Ifrane (6D) is a mountain town with green-tile roofs, skiing, and Morocco's most modern university. Azrou (6D) is a small Berber market town at the strategic crossroads of the northern and southern trade routes. The best times to visit are April to mid-June, September, and October. Summer inland is scorching; winter can be cool and rainy.

Fez, the best-preserved medieval city of the Arab-Islamic world and the starting point for excursions into the Middle Atlas, is three cities in one. Spread across the heart of the Fez River valley is the original 9th-century Fez el Bali, or Ancient Fez. Fez el Djedid, or New Fez, added in the 13th century, begins from Bab Boujeloud and rises up the valley to the 20th-century, French-built Ville Nouvelle, which lies apart, outside the ramparts.

The medina of Fez is a mysterious, intensely populated labyrinth, full of flourishing artisans and so many monuments it is hard to know where to begin.

THE INNER COURTYARDS (6C)
Fez the Mysterious p. 22

As late as the middle of this century, Christian foreigners could not penetrate the inner courtyards of Fez. Today although mosques are open only to Muslims, you can enter and explore Dar Batha Palace; walk around all the medersas; lunch at the Palais Mnebhi; peer undisturbed into Moulay Idriss's Mausoleum and the Kairaouine Mosque; and stay in a traditional house, La Maison Bleue. Its original Arab-Moorish decor—painted cedar ceilings, carved cedar doors, blue mosaics and tiles—is intact, and the suites are elegant and comfortable. Dinner is served in the brocade-draped lower salons, accompanied by an Andalusian lutenist.

CONTACT La Maison Bleue, 2 Place de l'Istiqlal Batha, 30000 Fez, tel. 05/74—18—43, fax 05/74—18—43, maisonbleue @fesnet.net.ma.

DISTANCES 289 km (179 mi) from Casablanca, 483 km (300 mi) from Marrakesh.

FACILITIES 6 deluxe suites, 4 junior suites, all with private bath. Restaurant, TV, air-conditioning, library, rooftop terrace.

PRICES Deluxe suite 2,500DH, junior suite 1,700DH, including Moroccan breakfast.

ANOTHER OPTION Riad Fes: Near the Hotel Palais Jamaï (*see* Fez the Knowable, *below*), this is a second *maison d'hôte* opened by the el Abbadi family, which runs La Maison Bleue. Rooms have mountain and medina views. Make reservations through La Maison Bleue. Guests check in at La Maison Bleue and are escorted to the house. There is no access by car. 6 suites, 3 rooms. Restaurant, Andalusian garden, panoramic bar and terrace, hammam. Double, high season 1,000DH; suite 2,000DH. Double, low season (July—Aug.) 800DH; suite 1,700DH. Meals 280DH.

SIGHTS IN THE SOUK (6C)
Fez the Knowable p. 26

The road around the northern ramparts runs right into the Hotel Palais Jamaï at Bab Jamaï. Watch out for hustlers on mopeds offering to show you the way: they'll take you the long way around and ask for a tip. The Palais Jamaï will arrange for an authorized guide for city tours. Built in the 19th century by the powerful brothers Jamaï, grand viziers to Sultan Moulay Hassan, the Arab-Moorish–style palace, with its panoramic view of Fez, was converted into a hotel in the 1930s. To walk to the souks, turn left outside the hotel, bear left, and descend to Place Nejjarine and the heart of Fez el Bali. The Nejjarine Souk—the carpenters' souk—is near the Nejjarine Fountain and the magnificently renovated Nejjarine Fondouk. Souk el Attarin—the spice market—is near the Kairaouine Mosque. On rue Cherabliyin are leather and *babouche* makers. The wool-dyers' souk is down past the Seffarine Medersa, just before the bridge. Visit the medieval-looking tanneries in the morning, when the pits are at their most colorful. That odor in the air is pigeon excrement, which is used in tanning. The potters' market, billowing with smoke from the kilns, is past Bab Ftouh. Hotel Palais Jamaï overlooks all of Fez. Most rooms have balconies and a medina, garden, or rampart view.

CONTACT Bab Guissa, 30000 Fez, tel. 05/63—43—31, fax 05/63—50—96.

DISTANCES 289 km (179 mi) from Casablanca, 483 km (300 mi) from Marrakesh.

FACILITIES 119 rooms, 15 suites. Moroccan and international restaurants, poolside grill, piano bar, pool, fitness center.

PRICES Double 2,100DH—2,300DH, with a rampart or medina view. Suite 5,000DH—18,000DH, depending on style. Buffet breakfast 150DH. Lunch and dinner 220DH—390DH.

ANOTHER OPTION Hôtel Splendid: If you want less expensive lodgings, try this hotel in the Ville Nouvelle. 9 rue Abdelkrim el-Kattabi, Fez, tel. 05/62—21—48, fax 05/65—48—92. 71 rooms. Restaurant, pool. Double 220DH, including breakfast and dinner.

VOLUBILIS, THE MIDDLE ATLAS (6C)
The Romans Remain p. 64

The French began excavation of Volubilis in 1915 but completed only 44 of the 110 acres. The bronze statues, marble columns, pottery, and jewels are housed in the Musée Archéologique in Rabat (4C). The Berbers called it Oualili; the Romans enlarged it as a granary for Rome. The Arabs, under Moulay Idriss, brought Islam and the first Arab dynasty to Morocco, founding the holy village of Moulay Idriss (6C), a couple of miles from Volubilis. In the 18th century, when Moulay Ismail reestablished Berber supremacy in the region, he was inspired by talk of Louis XIV's palace and wanted his new capital, Meknes (6C), to be as beautiful and immense as Versailles. His builders took stones from Volubilis to build Meknes. The region remains fertile, flourishing, and well populated and supplies all of Morocco with produce. The best time to visit is April to mid-June. The rambling Volubilis Inn overlooks the ruins and is the only hotel for miles around.

CONTACT Volubilis Inn, B.P. 20, Moulay Idriss, Zerhoun, tel. 05/54—44—05, fax 05/54—43—69.

DISTANCES 65 km (40 mi) from Fez, 255 km (158 mi) from Casablanca.

FACILITIES 50 rooms, 4 suites. 2 restaurants, terrace café, bar, garden, air-conditioning, TV, phone, 2 tennis courts, horseback riding.

PRICES Double, high season (late Dec.—early Jan., mid-Feb.—May, Sept.—mid-Nov.) 626DH—826DH. Double, low season (mid-Nov.—late Dec., early Jan.—mid-Feb., June—Aug.) 506DH—706DH. Suite 1,200DH—1,600DH. Prices depend on view (ruins or garden) and include breakfast and dinner. For nonguests, Continental breakfast is 48DH, Moroccan breakfast 90DH; other meals 170DH.

ANOTHER OPTION Hôtel Transatlantique: Opened in 1925, this is one of the five oldest hotels in Morocco. It was used as headquarters by World War II leaders, including Charles de Gaulle and Winston Churchill. Zankat El Meriniyine, Meknes, tel. 05/52—50—50, fax 05/52—00—57. 60 traditional-style rooms, 60 modern rooms. Restaurant, piano bar, air-conditioning, TV, phone, 2 swimming pools, 3 tennis courts, gardens, olive groves. Double 780DH, suite 1,620DH, including breakfast. Other meals 170DH and à la carte.

FEZ AND THE MIDDLE ATLAS HIGHLIGHTS

The Kairaouine Mosque, founded in 857 by a woman refugee from Kairouan in Tunisia, is the largest mosque in Morocco, and its university is one of the oldest in the world. It is said that Arab mathematics made their way from the university to Europe via Pope Sylvester II, who studied here in the 10th century. Enigmatic and unapproachable, the Kairaouine was the fountain of learning in Morocco. Today Fez is still regarded as the seat of learning by Moroccans. The Moulay Idriss II Mausoleum and the Nejjarine Fountain and Fondouk are especially well preserved, as is Dar Batha Palace, now a museum and venue for Fez's yearly Festival of Sacred Music. The Medersa Bou Inania is one of Morocco's most beautiful monuments, the best-preserved of the 14th-century Merenid Koranic schools (medersa means place of study). Like those of the Seffarine, Attarin, Cherratin, and Misbahiya medersas, its monklike cells were inhabited by Koranic students until the 1950s.

Some concerts in Fez's Festival of Sacred Music—held yearly in late May—take place in Volubilis. A widely celebrated religious festival is held every September in Moulay Idriss. Local hotels can provide you with information about the annual festivals, or contact the ONMT Fez.

THE ATLANTIC COAST

Morocco's Atlantic coastline stretches 3,200 km (2,000 mi) from Dakhla, near the border with Mauritania, where the Western Sahara slopes down to cliff-edged shores, up to Cap Spartel and the Straits of Gibraltar. All the way up are turquoise coastal waters with silver-sand beaches rising up into dunes, wild cliffs, headlands, and bluffs. Except for large seaside resorts such as Agadir, El Jadida, and Skhirat near Rabat and a handful of small ones such as Essaouira, Sidi Bouzid,

Oualidia, and Asilah, the beaches are unspoiled and unfrequented. In the 15th century the Atlantic Barbary Coast was one of the prime targets of the Portuguese as well as pirate fleets; the Portuguese conquered the ports from Agadir up to Tangier. Most were lost again to Moroccan rule 30 to 50 years later, but the Portuguese held Essaouira for 70 years, Tangier for more than 100, and El Jadida and Casablanca for 250. Pirates and buccaneers of all nationalities prospered for several centuries along the Barbary Coast. It wasn't until the 19th century that peace finally came to the area. The best time to visit the northern Atlantic coast is May through September; the south has good weather year-round.

ESSAOUIRA (2E)

Ports, Pirates, and the Portuguese p. 34

Between 1470 and 1541, the Portuguese held Essaouira—then called Mogador—as a strategic seaport. The town languished until the 18th century, when a major face-lift was administered by a French architect to impress European traders. British-born James Whaley created the enchanting Villa Maroc in 1990, renovating and joining three 18th-century houses just inside the ramparts. The hotel is famous for its indigo-and-white courtyard. Rooms and suites vary in size but all have a bright, airy seaside feel and are decorated with Moroccan handicrafts. Near the Skala, watch the *thuya* artists at work, and buy gifts from 30DH upward. In the port there are many great seafood grills.

CONTACT Villa Maroc, 10 rue A. Ben Yassine, Essaouira, tel. 04/47—31—47 or 04/47—67—58, fax 04/47—58—06 or 04/47—28—06, villa.maroc@casanet.net.ma.

DISTANCE 150 km (93 mi) from Marrakesh, 328 km (204 mi) from Casablanca.

FACILITIES 14 rooms, 2 with bath, 12 with shower. 4 suites, 4 junior suites, and 1 apartment, all with bath. The rooftop terrace suites are the favorites. 5 salons with fireplaces. Restaurant. Camel and horseback riding.

PRICES Double 610DH; junior suite for 2 people 780DH, for 4 people 1,000DH. Apartment for 4 people 1,200DH. Rates include breakfast. Dinner 160DH. Reserve 3 months in advance for rooms and the day before for meals.

ANOTHER OPTION Riad al Medina: This 18th-century palace was known as Hotel du Pacha in the '60s, when Jimi Hendrix and Frank Zappa popped in and out. 9 rue Attarine, 44000 Essaouira, tel. 04/47—59—07, fax 04/47—66—95. 5 rooms with bath, TV, phone. 20 suites with Moroccan salons. Double 664DH, suite 864DH—1,464DH, including breakfast. Dinner 150DH.

A SEASIDE DRIVE (2E–3D)
Beaches and Sea Bastions p. 58

The deserted, dune-edged beach of Diabat, next to Essaouira, is great for a quiet walk or picnic. There's an odd ruin by the sea that looks like a shipwreck but is a crumbling structure of Carthaginian origin. In El Oualidia, flamingo and Audoin's gulls can be seen around the blue lagoon. El Jadida is a pleasant, white-painted, seaside resort, popular in summer with Moroccans fleeing inland heat. The Hôtel Palais Andalous, once a pasha's palace, is full of Moorish tiles and plasterwork. The best time to visit is May through July.

CONTACT Hôtel Palais Andalous, Boulevard Docteur de la Lanouy, El Jadida, tel. 03/34—37—45, fax 03/35—16—90.

DISTANCES 170 km (106 mi) from Marrakesh, 333 km (207 mi) from Casablanca.

FACILITIES 28 rooms. Restaurant, courtyard bar. About 1¼ km (1 mi) from beach.

PRICES Double 300DH, including breakfast.

OTHER OPTIONS Auberge Tangaro: This inn is all white and cobalt blue. It has no electricity but overlooks the Diabat beach. The rustic yet elegant candlelit restaurant is surprisingly good. Quartier Diabat, B.P. 8, Essaouira, tel. 04/78—47—84 or 04/78—57—35, fax 04/48—02—29. 18 rooms with shower, 2 small duplex apartments. Restaurant.

Double 650DH, apartment double 800DH, including breakfast and dinner. **Hôtel Restaurant l'Arraignée Gourmande:** This charmer looks like a small private villa from the front. El Oualidia Plage, El Oualidia, tel. 03/36—64—47, fax 03/36—61—44. 5 rooms with shower. Lagoon and garden views. Double 250DH, breakfast 25DH/person. Double with breakfast and dinner 450DH. **Motel Club Hacienda:** This small place in Sidi Bouzid has a relaxed seaside atmosphere, a pool, a tennis court, and a café. Sidi Bouzid, El Jadida, tel. 03/34—83—11, fax 03/34—83—99. 10 apartments, 2—4 people in each. Double 300DH. **Royal Golf Hôtel d'el Jadida:** This luxury option is on an 18-hole golf course on a quiet coast road. Km 7, Route de Casablanca, Haouzia, tel. 03/35—41—42, fax 03/35—34—73. 115 rooms. Restaurant, pool. Double 900DH, including breakfast. Golf 300DH/person. **Aplanos Gallery and Maison d'Hôte:** Belgian art collector Anne-Judith van Loock and her husband, Ahmed Benraadiya, run this place in Asilah. 89 rue Tijara, 90050 Asilah, tel./fax 09/41—74—86. 3 suites and 3 apartments with bath and ocean views. 1 villa for weekly rental. Double suite or apartment 500DH, including breakfast. Renting the villa for a maximum of 10 people costs 3,000DH/week.

THE ATLANTIC COAST HIGHLIGHTS

Agadir (2G), once held by the Portuguese, is now held by sun-worshipping Germans and Brits. Essaouira's port and Skala, full of fishing nets and seagulls, look out over a curved beach and deserted sand dunes. **Safi** (2E) has no beach, but its well-preserved Portuguese Sea Castle and flourishing potters' market are worth a visit. The cobbled lanes of El Jadida's medina lead to the seaward ramparts. Today a quiet nostalgic stroll belies the town's long history as a fiercely held Portuguese port. El Jadida's beach is crowded, but nearby Sidi Bouzid is quiet and runs off into dunes. Farther up the coast is **Azemmour** (3D), another Portuguese fortress town, built beside Morocco's great Oum-er-Rbia river. Casablanca's Anfa district was also once held by the Portuguese. Today the colossal Mosque Hassan II, finished in 1993 after five years of devotional work, towers at the sea's edge like a holy beacon. Farther north, 40 km (25 mi) from Tangier, is the tiny, enclosed fishing village of **Asilah** (5A), with its Portuguese ramparts, narrow lanes of colorfully painted houses, and wide, sandy shore. It's refreshingly quiet and sleepy, except in August, when the yearly International Arts Festival takes place.

MARRAKESH

Encircled by crenellated, salmon-pink ramparts that protect its mysterious, labyrinthine medina, Marrakesh (3E) is the ancient heart of Morocco. Its exotic allure is a product of a unique blend of the races and cultures—Berber, Moorish, Arab, and African—that has characterized this desert city. The favorite capital of successive sultans, virtually unchanged since medieval times, Marrakesh is a boisterous, sandy oasis city. Lying on the Haouz Plain beneath the High Atlas mountains, it was once a strategic stop for camel caravans on their way north from fabled Timbuktu, and remains an enigma. Marrakesh is a city of contrasts and pervasive sensuality, where palaces and ornate mansions of unrivaled refinement and tranquillity stand beside clamoring bazaars and the Djemâa el Fna, with its snake charmers and African drums. Donkeys pull up alongside a Mercedes at traffic signs, and dry, dusty alleys give onto lush green courtyards. People fall instantly in love with Marrakesh: its openness, its blue skies, its endless sunshine, its palm trees, its colorful souks, and, most of all, the beguiling, unhurried rhythm that lies beneath and beyond the fast, disorderly traffic.

PALACES, COURTYARDS, AND GARDENS (3E)
Pearl of the South p. 40

Once a year, usually in early June, Palais El Badi comes to life as the National Festival of Popular Arts takes over the sunken orange gardens and the crumbling reception hall—once held up by 50 columns—with musicians and entertainers from all over Morocco. The palace belongs to the king and is used for his entourage. If you are in town when he is, you won't be permitted to visit. Maintained as a pleasure garden by sultans, the Menara pavilion and lagoon are secluded within vast olive and fruit orchards. La Mamounia Hotel began as a garden in the 18th century. The garden was a wedding gift from Sultan Mohammed ben Abdallah to his son, Sidi Mamoun. The peaceful courtyards of Marrakesh's maisons d'hôte are all original, but the water that fills their marble fountains no longer comes straight from the Atlas mountains. Restaurants with cool inner courtyards include El Yacout, Dar Marjana, Kasbah la Rotonda, Tobsil, and Stylia.

CONTACT La Mamounia Hotel, Avenue Bab Jedid, Medina, 40000 Marrakesh, tel. 04/44—89—91, fax 04/44—49—40, www.mamounia.com.

DISTANCES 238 km (148 mi) from Casablanca, 483 km (300 mi) from Fez.

FACILITIES 171 rooms, 20 suites, 25 junior suites, 5 villas with bath, air-conditioning, TV. 5 restaurants, piano bar, casino, nightclub.

PRICES Double, high season (late Dec.—early Jan., mid-Mar.—late May, Oct.) 3,000DH—4,600DH. Double, midseason (Nov.—late Dec., early Jan.—mid-Mar, late May—mid-June, mid-Sept.—late Sept.) 2,400DH—4,000DH. Double, low season (mid-June—mid-Sept.) 1,900DH—3,200DH. Prices depend on view. Junior suite 3,400DH—4,600DH. Suite 7,500DH—10,000DH. Prices depend on size and season. Villas for 6 people 20,000DH—30,000DH/night, depending on season.

OTHER OPTIONS El Yacout: For dinner at this fairy-tale palace make reservations well in advance, several months ahead if possible. 79 Sidi Ahmed Soussi, Medina, tel. 04/38—29—29 or 04/38—29—00, fax 04/38—25—38. **La Maison Arabe:** In this small hotel in the *riad* style, all rooms are built around a central courtyard with Moorish-style architecture and European furnishings. 1 Derb Assehbe, Bab Doukkala, Medina, Marrakesh, tel. 04/39—12—33, fax 04/44—37—15. Private pool in the Palmery. 6 rooms, 6 suites with TV. Double, high season (mid-Sept.—mid-June)

1,900DH—3,000DH; suite 2,800DH—3,500DH. Double, low season (rest of yr) 1,500DH—2,500DH; suite 2,300DH—3,000DH. **Dar El Farah:** This formal maison d'hôte near Palais El Badi has original decor and a small pool surrounded by palms. There's also a secluded terrace with great views. Riad Zitoun el Jedid, Medina, Marrakesh, tel. 04/44—10—19 or 04/43—15—60, fax 04/43—15—59. 5 rooms. Double and single 900DH, including breakfast. **Dar les Zomorrodes:** Here you'll find original carved doors and ceilings, quaint bedrooms, and bathrooms with a shiny tadlak finish. Rue de la Bahia, Medina, Marrakesh, tel. 04/44—10—19 or 04/43—15—60, fax 04/43—15—59. 4 rooms. Courtyard pool, sunny terrace. Weekly rental 5,625DH—9,375DH for 2—8 people. **Les Deux Tours:** This is series of villas in the Palmery. Set among luxuriant gardens, each has its own courtyard and pool. Douar Abiad, BP 513, La Palmerie de Marrakesh, Marrakesh Principal, tel. 04/32—95—27, fax 04/32—95—23. 24 units with air-conditioning. Pool, hammam. Double, high season (mid-Dec.—early Jan.) 2,000DH, suite 3,000DH. Double, middle season (early—late Nov., early Feb.—May, Sept.—Oct.) 1,750DH, suite 1,850. Double, low season (late Nov.—mid-Dec., early Jan.—early Feb., June—Aug.) 1,250DH, suite 1,850DH. Breakfast 80DH. Meals on request. **Palais Rhoul:** Greco-Roman columns surround a glitzy pool at this hostelry in a well-concealed tropical garden in the Palmery. Local fax 04/32—94—96. Make reservations via the Paris office: 237 Boulevard Pereire, 75017 Paris, tel. 01—45—72—13—00, fax 01—45—72—13—01. 3 suites, 7 rooms with air-conditioning. Restaurant, pool, tennis court, hammam. Double, high season (Apr.—July, Dec.) 3,040DH, suite 4,320DH. Double, low season (Aug.—Nov.) 1,760DH, suite 3,200DH. **Le Verger de l'Etoile Filante:** This enormous, rambling, salmon-pink house is like an English castle, an Italian villa, and a Moroccan kasbah all in one. Set amid gardens, with a mosaic-floored pool, it's the ultimate hideaway in the Palmery. Dar Abiad, Circuit de la Palmerie, Marrakesh, tel. 04/32—97—97, fax 04/32—97—98. Weekly rate for main villa (4 double suites) 61,750DH, including breakfast and dinner. For the Doll's House (4 double rooms) 37,050DH, including breakfast and dinner.

DJEMÂA EL FNA (3E)

Carnival Supreme p. 46

Djemâa El Fna, in the heart of the medina, is a magnet for Marrakshis and tourists alike. All the cafés encircling the square have terraces where you can watch the sun set; most charge an entry fee of a few dirhams. A front seat at Café de France gives a view across the square as far as the illuminated silhouette of the great 12th-century Koutoubia Mosque. The Hotel CTM, Café Glacier, and Café Argana also have excellent terraces for an evening's viewing. Go early for the best seats. All the alleys that flow into Djemâa el Fna contain colorful bazaars of pottery, fabrics, jewelry, slippers, caftans, and djellabas. A good tip for shopping: look around first, don't make eye contact or start chatting with vendors, and don't enter a store until you're ready to bargain. There are many small hotels in the alleys on the south side of Djemâa el Fna that are inexpensive, clean, and fun to stay in. Hôtel Le Gallia, the most popular, is just behind the post office. The hotel is decorated with tiles, flowers, and plants.

CONTACT Hôtel Le Gallia, 30 rue de la Recette, Medina, Marrakesh, tel. 04/44—59—13, fax 04/44—48—53.

DISTANCES 238 km (148 mi) from Casablanca, 483 km (300 mi) from Fez.

FACILITIES 24 rooms with air-conditioning. Rooftop terrace.

PRICES Double 270DH, including breakfast. Make reservations at least 2—3 months in advance.

OTHER OPTIONS Hôtel Essaouira: Peace Corps personnel stay in the ceramic-tiled rooms here when visiting Marrakesh. 3 Sidi Bouloukate, Medina, Marrakesh, tel. 04/44—38—05. 31 rooms with shared bath. Rooftop terrace. Double 108DH, including breakfast. **Hôtel Islane:** This is around the corner from Djemâa el Fna, opposite the Koutoubia Mosque. Some rooms have views of the mosque. 279 Avenue Mohammed V, Marrakesh, tel. 04/44—00—81, fax 04/44—00—85. 40 rooms with air-conditioning. Restaurants, pizzeria, bar. Double 275DH, including breakfast. **Hôtel Ali:** Adventurous travelers on a budget meet up here. Rue Moulay Ismail, Medina, Marrakesh, tel. 04/44—49—79, fax 04/44—05—22, hotelali@hotmail.com. 38 small rooms with shower, 7 rooms with shared shower. Computer room with 5 terminals. Restaurant. Double 120DH, including breakfast.

MOROCCAN STYLE (3E)
Riad Enija p. 8

A *riad* is the traditional house of the bourgeoisie. All the salons of the lower and upper floors are set around a central inner courtyard behind high, windowless walls. On a street called a *derb,* among the souks, the Riad Enija is the most relaxed and elegant of these maisons-d'hôtes riads. Just outside you can shop for souvenirs or stroll around town. The nearby olive market has pyramids of black, green, pink, and spiced olives that are, some say, the most delicious in the world. Riad Enija preserves the refined Moorish details so conducive to quiet and contemplation. Ursula Haldimann, the owner, has added some equally exquisite modern sculptures and fabrics that blend harmoniously. The vast courtyard is home to an owl, a falcon, and a family of tortoises. The inn is not far from the Djemâa el Fna, at the Café de France end.

CONTACT Ursula Haldimann, Rahba Laktima, Derb Mesfioui 9, Marrakesh, tel. 04/44—09—26, fax 04/44—27—00, riadenija@cybernet.net.ma.

DISTANCES 238 km (148 mi) from Casablanca, 483 km (300 mi) from Fez.

FACILITIES 2 rooms, 7 suites, all with terraces. Garden courtyard, outside dining, rooftop terrace for sunning and drinks. Moroccan and international cuisine.

PRICE Double rooms 2,500DH, double suite 2,800DH, including breakfast. Extra bed 300DH. Children under 10 free. Meals 80DH—380DH/person.

A SENSUAL ART (3E)
For the Love of Henna p. 52

Djemâa el Fna has a row of highly competitive henna artists, on the Café Argana side. Veiled and wearing djellabas, they charge tourists what they can. Check out the price before going ahead. It's generally about 20DH for one anklet or bracelet, and 50DH—100DH for both hands, depending on how complicated the design is and whether the palms and/or the backs of the hands are done. For hotel calls, expect to pay more, 100DH—200DH, depending on how much henna you want and in which hotel you are staying. The designs are protected with a paste of lemon juice, sugar, and water covered with cotton. You must leave the paste on overnight for the darkest results.

CONTACT Most hotels can bring in a henna artist for you. The beauty salon or the hammam at La Mamounia Hotel is the most luxurious place to have henna applied. Riad Enija can also arrange for a henna artist, or you can choose your own from the artists in Djemâa el Fna.

MARRAKESH HIGHLIGHTS
The 16th-century Saadian Tombs in the southern medina lie partly in an ornate cedar-carved mausoleum and partly in a serene garden. The 19th-century Dar Si Said is a bijou mansion with a beautiful garden courtyard that is now home to a striking collection of antique Moroccan handicrafts. In the northern medina the somber but exquisitely detailed Ali ben Youssef Medersa has a sunlit central courtyard, and nearby is the Koubba Ba'adiyn, the only remaining Almoravid monument, revealing the palm and pine cone motifs that influenced later dynasties. Orange groves surround the great Koutoubia Mosque, 20 minutes away on foot at the far end of Djemâa el Fna on Avenue Mohammed V. From there, it's another half hour to Avenue Yacoub el Mansour in Gueliz, where you will find Le Jardin Majorelle, a lush, secluded garden with electric-blue gazebos, a creation of the painter Louis Majorelle that is now owned by Yves St. Laurent. Also worth seeing, 10 minutes' drive from the city on the road to

Casablanca, is the Palmery; the road winding through it gives glimpses of small farms and palatial villas among the date palms.

THE HIGH ATLAS

Stretching down from the Middle Atlas to the Atlantic coast, the huge High Atlas mountains slash southwest across Morocco, dividing it into two countries—the cool, fertile north and the hot, arid south. Stunningly snow-capped from November through March, the High Atlas rise from the Haouz plain 20 km (12 mi) south of Marrakesh, with good roads—but no guardrails—leading through the Tizi-n-Test and Tizi-n-Tichka passes to the pre-Saharan cities of Taroudant and Ouarzazate. There's also a network of negotiable rural roads. Inside the magnificent ranges is a mountain realm that civilization has barely touched, a feudal kingdom of Berber tribes who, before the French subjugated them and built roads, controlled access from Marrakesh to the south by the Tizi-n-Test and Tizi-n-Tichka, passes. Footpaths that are passable year-round as well as mule trails lead through the most beautiful mountain scenery in Morocco; you can overnight in refuges or in the mud-walled homes of the Berbers, who are known for their warmth and hospitality. The best months to hike are April, May, September, and October. Roads can be blocked by snow in winter.

THE GREEN VALLEY OF AÏT BOU GMEZ, DAR ITRANE (5E–F)
The Descendants of Gmez p. 42

This paradisical valley is one of the most remote in the High Atlas, beneath the Irhil M'Goun range, which is 19 km (12 mi) long and the second-highest in Morocco after Toubkal. You can spend days rambling among the valley's peaceful hamlets, visiting with the friendly inhabitants, and checking out the painted ceilings of their homes with a guide from Dar Itrane (a small, discreet donation might encourage them to preserve the ceilings). Nearby Zaouia Ahanesal (5E) is a holy village founded by a descendant of the Prophet Mohammed, Sidi Said Ahanesal, who was the first of a line of living saints called *agurram,* known as the Hansalia religious order. From Aït Bou Gmez there are many treks that require porters and mules. The main trek, requiring four or five days, is south through the Mgoun canyon to the Dadès Valley and El Kelâa M'Gouna (5F). Toward Azilal (4E) are the extraordinary Cascades d'Ouzoud, a series of falls that tumble more than 300 ft among carob, oak, and pomegranate trees into natural pools that are good for swimming.

CONTACT Dar Itrane, Bernard Fabry, Atlas Sahara Trek, 6 bis rue Houdhoud, Quartier Majorelle, Marrekesh, tel. 04/31—39—01, fax 04/31—39—05, sahara@cybernet.net.ma.

DISTANCES 325 km (202 mi) from Casablanca, 405 km (252 mi) from Fez.

FACILITIES 10 rooms with adjacent shared showers, 1 room with private shower. Dining room and terrace with valley views.

PRICE Double 360DH—420DH, including breakfast and dinner, depending on room size.

DRIVING THROUGH THE TIZI-N-TEST (3F)
Over the Top p. 30

If the pass is blocked with snow, a sign is posted just outside Marrakesh. If not, continue on your adventure. On the Taroudant road, just past Asni, a narrow road leads up past green mountain terraces of almond trees, past Luciano Tempo's folly, Kasbah Tamadot, to the stony village of Imlil, still signposted KUNDUN, for Martin Scorsese's film. Near Ijoukak there's a challenging climb, or you can take the long backroad piste to the imperious Kasbah Talat-n-Yacoub, also a location for many films. A few miles farther, walk around the ancient, roofless Tin Mal Mosque. Your journey ends in Taroudant (2G) at the Palais Salam, a 16th-century pasha's residence that uses the city's thick ramparts as its outer walls. The keyhole-shape pool lies beneath the ramparts, surrounded by bougainvillea and palm trees.

CONTACT Palais Salam, Avenue Moulay Ismail, B.P. 258, 83000 Taroudant, tel. 08/85—23—12, fax 08/85—26—54.

DISTANCES 223 km (138 mi) from Marrakesh, 461 km (286 mi) from Casablanca.

FACILITIES 95 rooms, 35 suites, all with traditional Moroccan decor, air-conditioning, TV, phone. 2 restaurants, bar, Moroccan salon, 2 pools.

PRICES Double, high season (late Dec.—early Jan., Mar.—June) 606DH—1,090DH. Double, low season (Nov.—late Dec., early Jan.—Feb., June—Oct.) 530DH—859DH. Price varies from old to new wing and from Riad I to Riad II. Rates include breakfast. Suites 1,410DH. Meals 130DH—150DH.

CAR RENTAL Europcar, 63 Boulevard Zerktouni, Marrakesh, tel. 04/43—12—28, fax 04/43—27—69.

OTHER OPTIONS La Residence de la Roseraie: This 54-acre idyll of roses is in Ouirgane. 60 km Route, Taroudant, tel. 08/43—20—94, fax 08/43—20—95. 14 rooms, 5 senior suites, 16 junior suites. Pool, bar, rustic dining room with log fire, trekking, horses to rent. Double 850DH; suites 1,000DH—1,250DH, including breakfast and dinner. **Au Sanglier qui Fume:** A French family runs this place 300 ft from La Residence de la Roseraie. C.P. 42150, Ouirgane, 61 km Route, Taroudant, tel. 08/48—57—07 or 08/48—57—08, fax 08/48—57—09. 15 rooms, 4 suites. Restaurant, bar, garden, mountain bikes, trekking excursions. Double 200DH—250DH, including breakfast; 460DH—510DH, including breakfast and dinner. Suite 350DH—450DH, including breakfast; 610DH—650DH, including breakfast and dinner. **La Gazelle d'Or:** Built in 1948, this former hunting lodge of a French baron is set in 25 acres of gardens. B.P. 60, Taroudant, tel. 08/85—20—39, fax 08/85—27—37. 40 pavilions with air-conditioning, TV. Tented dining room, pool, tennis courts, horseback riding. Double 3,430DH; suite 4,424DH—7,529DH, including breakfast and dinner.

LAND OF THE IDA OUTANANE, HÔTEL DES CASCADES (2F)

Paradise Valley p. 70

British hippies put Paradise Valley on the map when they camped here in the 1960s. The road through the valley twists upward through the mud villages of Tamarout, Tidili, and Tiskji. The waterfalls lie below the hotel, among almond trees. They're reachable on foot and are best seen in spring, as they are used later in the year for irrigation. From the village of Immouzer, take the road down from the square, then to the left. "Guides" and trinket sellers wait for tourists under the olive trees; just pass on by. There's a trek back up from the village to the hotel that cuts through the cliffs, as well as treks by mule and overnights in Berber hamlets unreachable by road. A gardener's delight, full of cool arbors and shady bowers, the Hôtel des Cascades is owned by Jamal Eddine Atbir, whose father opened it with just 3 rooms 20 years ago.

CONTACT Jamal Eddine Atbir, Hôtel des Cascades, Immouzer des Ida Outanane, Agadir, tel. 08/82—60—12 or 08/82—60—23, fax 08/82—16—71.

DISTANCES 571 km (355 mi) from Casablanca, 316 km (196 mi) from Marrakesh.

FACILITIES 27 rooms with bath and private terrace. Restaurant, pool, children's pool, tennis court. Terrace for breakfast, cocktails, and barbecues.

PRICE Double 600DH, including breakfast.

HIGHLIGHTS OF THE HIGH ATLAS

The road through the Tizi-n-Tichka pass to **Ouarzazate** (4F) is almost as spectacular as the Tizi-n-Test road. The remote, elaborate **Kasbah Telouet** (4F), not far from the pass, makes a great pit stop. The entire High Atlas are full of treks, well-organized and led by local guides. The trip to Toubkal National Park is one of the most popular, with endless peaks and remote Berber villages. **Djebel Toubkal** (3F; 13,750 ft) is the highest peak in North Africa; its summit is accessible. Asni, Imlil, and Ouirgane are good starting points—with mules, guides, porters, and cooks for hire. A less energetic hike is through the Imlil to Aroumd, or Asni to Tachdirt, valleys. In summer the **Ourika Valley** (3F) is the favorite haunt of Marrakshis seeking respite from the heat, and in winter there's good skiing on the slopes of **Djebel Oukaimeden** (3F).

THE SOUTH

The South is all the territory lying south of the High and Middle Atlas mountain ranges, from Agadir in the west across to Er-Rachidia in the east. The land is mostly arid and sandy, but there are three river valleys (the Drâa, the Dadès, and the Ziz) with settlements and lush oasis gardens, and pisé kasbahs of all sizes and shapes, inhabited and abandoned. Kasbahs abound all over Morocco, but they are synonymous with the South and are found from Tafraoute in the Anti-Atlas to Erfoud on the Sahara's edge. The South finishes where the Sahara starts, at the border with Algeria. The Deep South is the sparsely populated region from Guelmim (1H) down through the Western Sahara (reclaimed from the Spanish in 1975) to the coastal city of Dakhla. The best time to visit is April through May. Summer is mighty hot, and winter can be overcast.

THE LAND OF MUD CASTLES (4–5 F)

Kasbah Country p. 20

Kasbahs take many forms, from a one-family feudal fortress to the protected center of a village, town, or city. They usually have tribal ornamentation on their turrets and crenellations. A *ksar* is an enclave for a whole community, less fortified and less ornate. The area from Ouarzazate along the Dadès Valley and up into Dadès Gorge lives up to its name, Valley of a Thousand Kasbahs. Since the 1930s the South has provided endless desert locations for movies, including *The Man Who Knew Too Much, Lawrence of Arabia,* and *Patton.* The kasbah-style Riad Salam Hotel in Ouarzazate is cool, private, and peaceful. Its unpretentiousness and manager Mohammed Benjedot's friendly diplomacy make the hotel a popular hideaway for ambassadors, ministers, and celebrities.

CONTACT Riad Salam Hotel, Avenue Mohammed V, Ouarzazate, tel. 04/88–33–35, fax 04/88–27–66.

DISTANCES 204 km (127 mi) from Marrakesh, 434 km (270 mi) from Casablanca.

FACILITIES 45 rooms, 17 suites with air-conditioning, TV. Restaurant, bar, pool, 4 tennis courts, horseback riding. Guides, excursions.

PRICES Double 400DH–800DH, suite 800DH–1,200DH. Breakfast 70DH. Other meals 150DH.

OTHER OPTIONS Berbere Palace: This hotel is large and somewhat glitzy. Rooms are in villas surrounded by gardens. Quartier Mansour Eddhabi, Ouarzazate, tel. 04/88–30–77, fax 04/88–30–71. 214 rooms, 8 suites with air-conditioning, TV. Restaurant, bar, pool, tennis court, hammam. Double 900DH–1,500DH, suite 2,000DH–7,000DH. Breakfast 90DH. Other meals 170DH–210DH. **Hôtel La Kasbah:** This overlooks Aït Ben Haddou. Complexe Touristique, Ait Ben Haddou, Ouarzazate, tel. 04/89–03–02 or 04/89–03–08, fax 04/88–37–87. 41 rooms, 30 with shower; others share bath. Restaurant, bar, pool. Double 180DH, including breakfast. Other meals 80DH–110DH. **Hôtel Kasbah de la Vallée:** The best of the many simple inns is by the river, 27 km (15 mi) into Dadès Gorge. Tel. 04/83–17–17. 22 rooms with shower. Rooftop terrace areas and Berber-tent sleeping. Double 80DH–150DH. Meals 70DH.

THE MOUSSEM OF EL KELÂA M'GOUNA (5 F)

Ode to a Rose p. 36

The *moussem* is a three-day celebration of the rose harvest. Once upon a time it took place spontaneously, as and when the locals saw fit, with stalls, folklore, and a horse fantasia on red carpets in the streets. These days it is organized by the tourist office, and takes place in the town's arena at scheduled hours. The Capp Florale distillery is on the main street, at the eastern end of town; anyone will point it out. Don't be dissuaded if a distillery guardian seems not to understand your request for a tour. Only a few visitors are allowed in at a time, so try again later. The ONMT in New York can tell you—albeit at the last moment—the dates and program for the festival, which is dependent on when the roses are in bloom. During the moussem, inquire at the ONMT tent, 300 ft past the distillery, for days and hours of the celebration. Run by nomadic Frenchman Jean-Pierre Capel, the Auberge Rosa Damaskina is full of flowers and charm, a welcome respite after a day of clamorous celebrations.

CONTACT Auberge Rosa Damaskina, B.P. 178, El Kelâa M'Gouna, tel. 04/83—69—13, fax 04/83—69—69.

DISTANCES 296 km (184 mi) from Marrakesh, 525 km (326 mi) from Casablanca.

FACILITIES 5 rooms with private shower, 5 share shower. Dining is available in a caidal tent, in a Moroccan salon, or on the river terrace.

PRICES Double 150DH—211DH. Breakfast 26DH. Other meals 98DH.

OTHER OPTION Hôtel les Roses du Dadès: This kasbah-style inn is a 15-minute walk uphill from the town center. It has a restaurant, but you'll find better food on the main street at the two cafés, where all the foreigners go. B.P. 196, El Kelâa M'Gouna, tel. 04/83—63—36, fax 04/83-60—07. 100 rooms, 2 suites, all with bath or shower and air-conditioning. Restaurant, bar, pool, terrace café with mountain views. Double 300DH, suite 500DH. Breakfast 40DH.

ZAGORA (5G)

A Date in the Oasis p. 66

On the barren, lunar-landscape road south from Ouarzazate is the small town of Agdz, with its impressive Kasbah Tagersift. The inhabitants will show you around. From here to Zagora, along the River Drâa and the 95 km (59 mi) of oasis, are kasbahs of all sizes, including Tamnougalte, Tinzouline, and Igdaoun. Zagora itself is just a small market settlement, with one bustling main street, at the center of one of the most productive date-palm oases in Morocco. About 20 km (12 mi) south of Zagora is the holy village of Tamegroute where an aged librarian watches over ancient gazelle-skin manuscripts. Next door you can visit the 11th-century Sufi Naciri *zaouia,* a refuge for sick souls. A few minutes away are the dunes of Tinfou and the small,

whimsical kasbah Auberge du Sable, owned by a family of Moroccan artists. It's a desert art gallery, all sandy walls, pots, and paintings. The road from Tinfou to Mhamid runs through deserted, dramatic hamada terrain, and the awesome Beni Selmane pass. There are several simple café-restaurant-auberges around Mhamid where you can stop for meals and refreshments. After Mhamid the paved road ends.

CONTACT La Fibule du Drâa, B.P. 11, 45900 Zagora, tel. 04/84—73—18 or 04/84—73—23, fax 04/84—72—71, fibule@atlasnet.net.ma.

DISTANCES 397 km (247 mi) from Marrakesh, 635 km (394 mi) from Casablanca.

FACILITIES 30 rooms with bath and air-conditioning. Restaurant, bar, garden, pool. Camel-trekking excursions with overnights in Mhamid can be arranged. There are divan accommodations in a communal salon for the young and/or adventurous.

PRICES Double 360DH—640DH, including breakfast. Divan in salon with communal shower 160DH person. Low-season (most of Jan., June—late Dec.) rates 15% less. Meals 85DH. Make reservations 2—3 months in advance.

OTHER OPTIONS Ksar Tinsouline: The owner of La Fibule du Drâa runs this pleasant hotel. Avenue Hassan II, 45900 Zagora, tel. 04/84—72—52, fax 04/84—70—42, fibule@atlasnet.net.ma. 90 rooms, 10 suites. Restaurant, pool. Double 545DH, suite 900DH—1,800DH for 2—4 people, including breakfast. Other meals 120DH. **Kasbah Asmaa:** This is across the river, inside the oasis. B.P. 78, Zagora, tel. 04/84—72—41, fax 04/84—75—27. 38 rooms. Pool, dining in caidal tent, excursions. Double 300DH. Breakfast 30DH. Other meals 90DH.

HIGHLIGHTS OF THE SOUTH

Ouarzazate (4F) is the gateway to the South, as well as the hub of the Moroccan movie industry. Its fairy-tale Kasbah Taourirt is a prime location for desert fantasies. From Ouarzazate to **Boumalne** (5F) there's an impressive array of kasbahs in various stages of crumbling. **Ben Moro** and

Amerhidil (4F) are the best-preserved, much celebrated on celluloid as archetypal *Arabian Nights* palaces. Tinerhir has a lush oasis garden fed by a river whose source is in the cliffs of the Todra Gorge. The Taourirt and Tiffoultoute kasbahs in Ouarzazate are among those built in the 19th century by the Glaoui family to control the Southern Berber tribes.

THE ANTI-ATLAS

The Anti-Atlas mountains are a vast, arid, sparsely populated landscape of sandstone ridges that swirl southwest from Ouarzazate to the Atlantic coast. In addition to Tafraoute and Tiznit (1G), main towns include Tazenacht (4G), where there is a women's carpet-making cooperative, and Taliouine (3G), known for its saffron and Glaoui Kasbah. There are a few camel herders and small oasis settlements such as Tata (3G), Akka (2G), and Foum el Hassan (2H), known as the Tata loop. The best time to visit this region is April through June before the midsummer heat. In spite of the southern location, winter can be cool with occasional rain.

TAFRAOUTE AND THE AMELN VALLEY (2G)
The Pink Wild West p. 54

You can explore all of the 26 hamlets crouched in the Ameln Valley undisturbed. In mid-February they are a picture of pink and white almond blossoms. Otherwise the only vegetation is the hardy argan tree, famous for its nutty golden oil, extracted by the local women. Buy some at the Wednesday souk for 30DH a bottle. From Tafraoute you can exert yourself with a hike up Djebel el Kest (2G), or take a 20-minute walk from the Hôtel les Amandiers to see the prehistoric painted gazelle. On the road to Tiznit (1G) is the Hôtel Kerdous, worth a stop for its views of Kerdous Pass.

CONTACT Hôtel Les Amandiers, B.P. 10, Tafraoute, tel. 08/80—00—08 or 08/80—00—88, fax 08/80—03—43.

DISTANCES 450 km (279 mi) from Marrakesh, 624 km (387 mi) from Casablanca.

FACILITIES 58 rooms with shower or bath, air-conditioning, TV, phone. Restaurant, bar, pool. You'll find better food at the simple Restaurant Marrakesh on rue Tariq en Nahzi, down from the main square.

PRICES Double, high season (Apr.—May, Oct., late Dec.) 700DH. Double, low season (rest of yr) 500DH. Breakfast 40DH.

ANOTHER OPTION Hôtel Kerdous: This renovated kasbah is at 3,300 ft. Col du Kerdous, Km 54, Route de Tiznit à Tafraoute, B.P. 326, Tiznit, tel. 08/86—20—63, fax 08/86—28—35. 35 rooms. 2 restaurants, bar, pool. Double 650DH, including breakfast. Other meals 120DH.

HIGHLIGHTS OF THE ANTI-ATLAS

Just outside **Taroudant** (2G) is Kasbah Tioute, now a luxury Moroccan restaurant. In 1952 Yul Brynner filmed *Ali Baba and the Forty Thieves* here. Twenty-five miles south of Aït Bahia, perched on an erupting mount, is Kasbah Tioute. Climb up and you'll meet the last aged members of the Ida ou Gnidif tribe. Nineteenth-century **Tiznit** (1G) has intact salmon-pink ramparts and a good silver souk. Typical Anti-Atlas oases include **Tleta n'Tagmout** (2H), where the mountains are green and pink; **Foum el Hassan** (2G), whose series of antelope rock carvings dates from 2000 BC; and **Figuig** (9E)—once a stopover for pilgrims on their way to Mecca and a flourishing date-palm oasis for hundreds of years—reached by a spectacularly isolated but negotiable 400-km (248-mi) road through red-tinged mountains.

THE SAHARA

The Sahara (the word means hot and dry in Arabic) begins with arid sandstone mountains and sandy plains, like the burnished and desolate Sarhro and Bani ranges. Farther south the mountains disappear and the plains become vast stretches of hamada in which a rare palm-filled oasis settlement springs up here and there. The Moroccan Sahara stretches from Dakhla (6H), just above the Tropic of Cancer in the southwest, to Figuig (9E) on the Algerian border in the east. Desert settlements and oasis villages dot the region, and the hamada stretches down to Morocco's borders with Mauritania and Algeria. The best place to get an idea of the Sahara is around Merzouga (6F), reached by one of the hamada pistes from Erfoud or Rissani (6F). Until recently Merzouga had only one rough auberge; now, in response to the tourist demand for overnight accommodations in the desert, a cluster has sprung up. Locals try to lure visitors to their own inns by taking down the signs of others or by insisting that the inn you're looking for is closed. Ksar Sania (6F) is worth the hot drive and obstacle course. The best time to go to the desert is from mid-March through May, when skies are bluest and heat lowest. Winter can be overcast.

SUNRISE AND SUNSET IN THE MERZOUGAN DUNES (6F)

A Desert Day and Night p. 12

The biggest dunes in Morocco are in Merzouga. Nearby Erfoud and Rissani are sandy, edge-of-the-Sahara outposts. Four-wheel-drive trips to Merzouga to see sunrise and sunset can be arranged from any hotel or agency in Erfoud. The area is also great for bird-watching: desert sparrows, Egyptian nightjars, Arabian bustards, desert warblers, and blue-cheeked bee eaters can all be seen. The pistes to Merzouga are hard going. If you don't rent a four-wheel-drive vehicle, use a car with high clearance. Ksar Sania is the farthest and best of the several auberges beside the dunes, 50 km (31 mi) from Erfoud, just south of Merzouga.

CONTACT Gérard and Françoise Thomazo, Ksar Sania, B.P. 4-52202, Merzouga, Errachidia, tel. 05/57—74—14, fax 05/57—72—30. 50 km (31 mi) from Erfoud; directions given with reservation.

DISTANCES 584 km (363 mi) from Marrakesh, 822 km (510 mi) from Casablanca.

FACILITIES 16 dome-shape units with private showers and rooftop terraces. 8 rooms in the main building with exterior shower complex. Restaurant, communal tents, campsite.

PRICES Double 200DH, including breakfast and dinner. 25DH/person for tents. Double overnight in fibule 600DH.

OTHER OPTIONS Auberge Kasbah Derkaoua: This is 25 km (15 mi) from Erfoud. B.P. 64, Erfoud, Province Er-Rachidia, tel./fax 05/57—71—40. 14 rooms. Restaurant, pool. Double 400DH, including breakfast and dinner. Excursions to dunes and camel rides are available. **Atlas Sahara Trek:** Here you'll find a variety of deluxe desert trips. 6 bis rue Houdhoud, Quartier Majorelle, Marrekesh, tel. 04/31—39—01, fax 04/31—39—05, sahara@cybernet.net.ma.

HIGHLIGHTS OF THE SAHARA

Dakhla (6H), **Layoune** (7G), and **Tan-Tan** (7G) are modern Western Sahara coastal cities with plenty of dunes. The road south from Zagora runs through Tagounite and ends in Mhamid and Oulad Driss, in an area of sand dunes used for overnights in tents. Erfoud has a slow, desert-outpost ambience and a colorful date festival in October, when hundreds of varieties of dates are offered. Rissani is dustier and has the crumbling Sijilmassa ruins.

A native of Brighton, England, Pamela Windo came to the United States in 1979 and moved to Morocco in 1989, where she taught English to the children of the governor of Tiznit and wrote for the *Marrakech Echo* and *British Airways Magazine*. As a publicist for tourism in Morocco, she was later chosen by the Moroccan ambassador to the United Nations to present Morocco to the U.N. community, and she was location assistant to Martin Scorsese in the Ouarzazate-based filming of *Kundun*. Since returning to the United States, Windo has written for the *New York Daily News* and British *Condé Nast Traveller*.

British photographer Simon Russell, who currently lives in New York City, became fascinated with photography at the age of 19, when his mother, Pamela Windo, gave him his first camera. In 1990, a journey to Morocco to photograph the country's gardens and oases resulted in his first sale. Since then, he's worked for Royal Air Maroc, the Moroccan Tourist Board, and numerous hotels and restaurants. His photographs have also been published in *Hemispheres*, *Condé Nast Traveler*, *Travel Weekly*, and the *New York Daily News*.